You're *not* Crazy

Overcoming Parent/Child Alienation

Lynn Steinberg, Ph.D.

Dedication

This book is dedicated to all:

Alienated Parents
Alienated Grandparents
Alienated Extended Family

Alienated Children
Alienated Adult Children

And most especially to my beloved daughters
Ariel and Shay

Foreword

*C*ongratulations to Dr. Steinberg on her unique contribution to our knowledge of the phenomenon of parental alienation. In simple language, she captures the process of alienation and the roles played by each family member: the alienator, the alienated parent, and the child. Her examples are so vivid that the reader experiences the alienation as it is happening in the family. This is because Dr. Steinberg is a beautiful writer and an outstanding clinician who knows parental alienation inside and out.

The range of material covered in this book is far reaching. The reader will learn about the role of hatred in each member of the alienation triad, how parental alienation is both child abuse and parent abuse by the alienator, how the alienated child and alienated parent are both traumatized by this process, what happens to the alienated child's guilt and shame towards the alienated parent, and how the child is loved by the alienated parent but often serves as a mere possession or object for the alienator. The alienator's goal is to annihilate the other parent and rewrite the family narrative so that the child is no longer allowed to experience the loving connection between themselves and the alienated parent. The alienator goes so far as to turn the alienated parent's family against the alienated parent, stripping the alienated parent of their connection to important family members and support systems. Even in the face of this systemic psychic murder of the alienated parent, Dr. Steinberg is able to offer hope and help to the alienated parent, and hope to the alienated child, that both of them can eventually escape from the destructive and manipulative attacks and strategies of the alienator. She introduces a chapter by Dr. Melanie Funes which explores a topic rarely discussed, the experience of the new partner of the alienated parent and how the partner can be most helpful to the alienated parent.

Integrated into this book is discussion of the court experience for the alienated parent, the research literature and theoretical contributions to the field of parental alienation, and policy advances both internationally and by states in the United States which acknowledge parental alienation as child abuse. But let us not forget the abuse and cruelty towards the alienated parent, which courts and society at large still fail to understand and address effectively.

Linda Gunsberg, Ph.D.
Chair, Washington Square Institute Family Law
and Family Forensics Training Program,
New York (1997-2020)
Editorial Board, Psychoanalytic Inquiry
Private Practice, New York City

Linda Gunsberg, Ph.D.
130 W. 56th St. (Fl. 2)
New York, NY 10019
Tel: 212.246.5506

Testimonials

Dr. Steinberg's book was written with the treatment of the child in mind. The alienated child, to be specific. Her goal is to make sure all parents see, recognize, and understand the warning signs within their marriage that might lead to the kind of conditions that engender parental alienation. With her extensive background as a licensed clinical counselor and thorough and extensive experience working to reunite alienated children with their targeted parent in the cozy office behind her house, and as an expert witness in parental alienation cases in countless courtrooms across the country, this book delivers a detailed and much needed road map on how to avoid the telltale signs of the rot that is parental alienation growing within marriages, severely transforming loving and adoring children into weapons wielded by an alienating parent against the other formerly loving and adequate parent in a high conflict divorce war that inevitably and tragically leads to severely damaged and traumatized children who grow into alienated adults. Some remain forever separated from that loving parent, always maintaining it was their decision but, as Dr. Steinberg so vividly and movingly describes, they prefer to remain trapped in this unambiguous and cold world constructed for them by their favored parent, the alienator.

This book is for anyone who wants to, is about to, or has already got married and wants to have children. It systematically lays out the pitfalls that might lead to a devoted and loving parent losing the children they helped create and to whom they promised a lifetime of devotion. It describes the insidious transformation of the alienator from a loving partner into a tyrant who will stop at nothing to remove the other parent from their children's lives.

You might think it could never happen to you and yours, that your relationship could and should be able to withstand anything. Dr. Steinberg's book helps you to recognize the warning signs before it's too late. It provides you with the resources that can be used in court should you be unlucky enough to have been alienated from your children, and the mental and emotional signposts to help you through the darkest of days. Written with the kind of love only an alienated parent has for their children, Dr. Steinberg's book is never too difficult to read, nor too long, nor too scientific. It is just right for any parent holding on to the relationship with their children before they vanish forever into the arctic cold of parental alienation.

Ron Berglas, M.Ed.
Chair, Parental Alienation Legislative Group
Alienated Parent

In this book, Dr. Steinberg provides a hopeful road map of positive action to combat parental alienation. For all families struggling with this nightmare and heartbreak it is a must-read.

Melanie Funes, Ph.D.
Partner of an alienated parent

Dr. Steinberg's insights into the underpinnings of parental alienation are truly valuable. I highly recommend this book for guidance on managing this devastating situation.

Deborah Shreffler
Reunited adult alienated child, target parent
Advocate for target parents and children
Facilitator for legislative reform

You're Not Crazy is a must-read for any parent dealing with alienation. Few people understand how crazy making it is to be alienated from their child. Dr. Lynn Steinberg understands. She empowers you with the practical coping tools and arms you with essential steps to fight back.

A Targeted Parent

First published by Ultimate World Publishing 2020
Copyright © 2020 Lynn Steinberg, Ph.D.

ISBN

Paperback: 978-1-922497-62-8
Ebook: 978-1-922497-63-5

Cover design: Ultimate World Publishing
Layout and typesetting: Ultimate World Publishing
Editor: Marinda Wilkinson
Cover image: Lightspring-Shutterstock.com

Ultimate World Publishing
Diamond Creek,
Victoria Australia 3089
www.writeabook.com.au

Contents

Disclaimer

*T*here is a plethora of textbooks and journal articles on the subject of parental alienation for professionals, alienated parents, and children, many of which are listed in the Further Reading section at the back of this book. The Parental Alienation Study Group (PASG) has compiled a comprehensive list of books written on the topic. Many of these books and articles are based on scientific studies that have been conducted over the years regarding the statistics, law, symptomology, and treatment of parental alienation. In no way is this book intended to substitute what is stated in these remarkable works, as some of them are.

Who Is This Book For?

*J*udges, family law attorneys, Guardians Ad Litem, Department of Child and Family Services, psychologists, psychotherapists, family, and friends who are not familiar with the dynamics of parent alienation. Even if one thinks he/she is familiar with parental alienation, this book is intended to bring awareness that alienation is emotional abuse and should be treated as such. Alienation is far too prevalent and needs to be addressed. The damage it does to children is detrimental to their psyches and has a profoundly negative effect on their adult relationships.

For alienated parents, this book is intended to assist you in understanding what parental alienation is and how to get help from qualified professionals. The information that follows comes directly from the questions I am asked daily by panicked parents who have either just realized they are being alienated, or have been targeted for some time, and are fearful of losing their children for good.

I have endeavored to answer the common questions, provide useful and empowering advice and hopefully ward off the devastation that parental alienation so often brings.

Introduction

"The evolution of culture is ultimately determined by the amount of love, understanding, and freedom experienced by its children, because only love produces the self-integration and individuation needed for cultural innovation. Every abandonment, every betrayal, every hateful act towards children returns tenfold a few decades later upon the historical stage."

– Lloyd de Mause

*I*n the first scene of the movie *Equalizer 2*, Denzel Washington enters a dining car on a train headed for Turkey. He asks the barman for a cup of tea, but is told the bar is closed. A group of nasty-looking heavies are seated in the car, and one of them turns and orders the barman to serve Denzel. The man then sits down next to Denzel at the bar and tells him he can find whatever he wishes in Turkey, to which Denzel replies, "How about a man who kidnapped his own daughter and took her away from her

American mother? An abusive man, not a real man, with no love for the child, just a need to punish his ex-wife to take the one thing away from her that meant everything to her, with no intention of returning the child. Do you think I could find that man in Turkey?"

The kidnapper represented here is what you might call an extreme form of a parental alienator. A shoot-out ensues with the henchmen, and ends after Denzel has killed them all, including the alienator. In the next scene, the mother is reunited with her little girl. Although there is plenty of extreme physical violence in that scene, it does represent the very real psychological violence that goes on in parental alienation. The devastating effects it has on children will be discussed.

Obviously, all alienated or targeted parents wish to be reunited with their alienated children. We wish we had a hero to rush in, rescue our children and return them safely to us, with our child as delighted to see us as we are to see them. In real life, however, the alienators are more devious and there is no one to rescue the children from their alienators. In real life, the children are frequently resentful about being "rescued" from the alienator and direct their hatred, (yes, hatred), toward the targeted (alienated) parent.

This book is to invite you, the alienated parent, to be your own hero. It will help you understand how and why parent alienation (PA) occurs, and arm you with the information you need to tackle the situation with confidence and clarity. You'll gain knowledge and insight, so you can think creatively and strategically, understand your choices, and put up the fight of your life to regain custody of your children.

You should also know that you do not have to do this alone. Along the way, support will come in the form of your alternative heroes: a lawyer who is well-informed in the ways of PA, an expert witness, and a reunification therapist to name a few. It is vital that you collaborate with only those that have an appropriate level of expertise, and who have an in-depth understanding of the counterintuitive nature of parental alienation. With the right team standing with you, you'll significantly increase the chances of reuniting with your child or children.

This book is also written to assist the professionals involved—court personnel, the psychological community, and social workers—to understand the dynamics and disastrous consequences of parental alienation. Through no fault of their own, many lack the insight and experience needed to recognize the symptoms of PA, and are ill-equipped to find a resolution that is in the best interests of the child. Unfortunately, in the USA, there is a lack of training in the recognition of parent alienation. In other countries, the presence of PA is not only recognized, but they have also created laws against this type of child abuse (the laws are presented in their entirety at the back of this book). Parental alienation is typically described as a child's rejection of a parent and many professionals assume the problem is the parent. In reality, the rejected parent is not the cause of the problem, but is, rather, a symptom of the child's pathological alignment to the other parent.

It is also a useful resource for friends and family. Like the professionals, they are often unable to identify that alienation is taking place, and can be prone to rush to judgment, without understanding and seeing the complete picture of what is taking place.

All of the involved parties should be aware that the alienator is a master manipulator. They are often themselves the child of divorced parents who were, in many cases, alienators too. An alienator will make false allegations against the targeted parent and brainwash their children to do the same. The alienating is generally the work of a vengeful ex-spouse, but the campaign often begins while the couple is still together, growing like a toxic wave, washing away any pretense at family unity. The alienators have also cunningly set the stage with family and friends, usually without the targeted parent being aware of what is going on behind the scenes, or frequently, right in front of their noses.

An alienated parent once described to me how her husband would start an argument in the car on the way to outings with friends. After he had provoked her to an almost insurmountable point, she succumbed and got very angry. When they arrived, she was still furious, only for her husband to lean over to hug and kiss her, saying in an unctuous tone of the knowingly victorious, "Let's have a nice time." For years after that she thought he was the bigger person because he could let things go. Later she would realize she had been manipulated to appear undesirable and angry to her friends, family, and later to those very people she would hope to employ in her favor, those selfsame lawyers, therapists, family evaluators, and others involved in the custody case. This is called gaslighting.

Parental alienation is not easily understood. In fact, it is frequently misunderstood. This is perhaps because it often seems "counterintuitive" as physician and parental alienation expert Dr. Steven G. Miller explains:

> *"Alienating parents tend to present well: targeted parents tend to present poorly. As a rule, alienating parents present with the Four C's. They are cool, calm, charming, and convincing. That is because effective alienators tend to be master manipulators . . . In contrast, the targeted parent tends to present with the Four A's. They are anxious, agitated, angry, and afraid. That is because they are trauma victims. They are attempting to manage a horrific family crisis, usually without success, often while being attacked by professionals who fail to recognize the counterintuitive issues. Indeed, non-specialists often get these cases backwards."*[1]

To this day, parent alienation is not easily accepted by the (mostly) uneducated and resistant professionals, as well as lay people. The statement the targeted parent hears most is, *"You must have done something to lose your child."*

---

[1] Steven G. Miller, "Why Do Specialists Say that Parental Alienation is Counterintuitive?" *Parental Alienation International* (May & July 2018).

The actual reply to that accusation is, "No, I haven't." The targeted parent tends to be the healthier one, who is willing to work with the other parent because they love their children more than the alienating parent is able. They want their children to have a relationship with both parents. In contrast, the alienating parent is determined to seek revenge for some imagined slight, and will hate the targeted parent to the extent that they are willing to sacrifice the mental health of their children to punish them. Though their alienating acts are orchestrated to hurt the targeted parent, in the process they cause great damage to the children too.

As German philosopher Arthur Schopenhauer observed in the 19th century, when a problem in society needs to be challenged, and a truth accepted, the need for transformation goes through three stages:

- In the first stage, the truth is met with derision, or ridicule.
- In the second stage, there is violent opposition.
- In the third stage, there is acceptance, and the change becomes obvious.

Interestingly, towards the end of the process, it is common for those who initially resisted to believe they were part of the change from the start. An example of this was seen in South Africa in 1990. Workers at a Mercedes-Benz automobile factory bought and manufactured a car for Nelson

Mandela as a gift upon his release from twenty-seven years in prison, and at the time, this was met with much ridicule and laughter by the white population. Fast forward to a few years later when Mandela was inaugurated as the first black president of South Africa, and the story of how the car came to be was related as a source of pride, not only by the Blacks, but the Whites too—who to this day, deny ever ridiculing the idea.

Throughout history, there are countless other examples of this process in action. When the gay and lesbian community first started fighting for their rights, they were ridiculed, just like the workers in South Africa. Up until that time, homosexuality had been considered a personality disorder, to be "treated" in what could be truly sadistic ways. Gay men and women committed suicide rather than continue to endure rejection by their own families and society. Recently, the Supreme Court made it illegal to discriminate against gay people and gave them equal rights under the law. They are finally able to marry and be recognized as an equal part of society. Now being gay or lesbian is considered mostly common place in the United States, and if asked, most people would say that they were for equality from the beginning.

At the time of writing, the undertaking to teach society about parental alienation and to make it a crime, has just passed the stage of derision. Now it is an all-out war. It is the fervent hope of all involved in this movement, that the lack of acceptance of this dynamic will be resolved and we will reach the stage of acceptance in the very near future.

There are a few countries (Denmark, Mexico, and Brazil) who have existing laws in place against parent alienation and have enacted legislation that enables immediate repercussions for acts of alienation. Some other countries are working hard to change the law. In the United States currently, there are groups doing important and vital work to raise awareness, and ratify state by state measures, and institute mandatory training and reporting for all involved professionals.

As Margaret Meade, the great American anthropologist and writer said:

"Never believe that a few caring people can't change the world.
For, indeed, that's all who ever have."

Chapter 1

This Is War

"For them to perceive the advantage of defeating the enemy, they must have their rewards."
— **Sun Tzu, The Art of War (written 2,500 years ago)**

*A*lienated parents do not want a war. They simply want to get out of a bad marriage. Most want to develop a situation where their children have both parents in their lives and the going back and forth is as seamless as possible. Experts agree that this is the best possible outcome for a child's mental health and well-being if their parents are divorced.

An extremely well-adjusted, hard-working and successful young woman I know shared with me that when her parents announced their intention to divorce, all the plans for the custody of the children were already in place. The father moved a block away, and the children moved seamlessly between the two parents. They had the usual feelings of anger and hurt, but when their father married his mistress, their mother did not encourage dissention nor did she take sides. She explained that sometimes people fall out of love, but both parents loved them and the new stepmother was an additional person in the family who would be taking care of them.

By contrast . . .

The above scenario is an example of the ideal situation for children of divorced parents—but unfortunately, it does not always play out that way. Sometimes, a parent feels aggrieved about the separation, and is determined to punish the other parent for leaving the marriage. They become fixated on revenge and understand that what would hurt the other parent most is having their children taken away from them.

They accomplish this scenario by continually communicating— overtly and covertly—to their children that their other parent is not able to take care of them and does not love them.

Furthermore, they tell children the targeted parent does not deserve them and compounds those false allegations with malicious allegations of abuse, domestic violence, abandonment, misconduct, drug abuse, mental illness, and more. The children, in order to mollify the alienating parent who is convincing them to hate the other parent, eventually capitulate to the pressure of the experience. Eventually they join in the campaign of hate and retribution against the abandoned parent.

This campaign is unremitting and frequently results in the targeted parent not seeing their children again for weeks, months, and in especially extreme cases, years. When the truth finally dawns on the children, they may move to reconcile with the alienated parent. This depends on what remaining hold the alienator still has over the children. They also suffer from extreme guilt once they recall all the ways they mistreated their targeted parent, for which they are not culpable. Regrettably, the guilt and shame they feel often prevents them from reaching out to their rejected parent at all.

Without professional intervention, there is no mediating, negotiating, begging, or reasoning that can stop this process. I was involved in a case where an alienator attacked his wife in her home and spent a night in jail. The bail was set at $20,000. He called his adult children to bail him out, proclaiming his innocence. When he appeared in court for a restraining order, he had in hand an affidavit from each daughter supporting him and asserting he was never violent and their mother was "always angry." When he was asked why he had involved his daughters, he replied, "This is war."

Take heed alienated parents. This is war. This book will show you how to prepare for this unasked for war and how to fight and win for the right to be in your children's lives.

In recent years, a group of concerned parents and citizens formed ParentalRights.org, with the aim to preserve and uphold parental rights in the Children and Family Courts through an amendment to the US Constitution. This is a timely response to a growing trend toward a misapplication of the "best interests of the child" principle. The reality of what can happen in court is, that the new human rights' application of the best interest of the child principle can be used to abolish the presumption of parental fitness. When applied in this way the **judicial prerogative to determine the child's best interest becomes the default, rather than a last resort reserved for when a parent has been proven unfit.** This means that a parents' private choices for their children can be called into question at any time a government personnel disagrees with them.

International law expert Geraldine Van Bueren describes, the ramifications of the application when used in this way:

"It provides the decision and policy makers with the authority to substitute their own decisions for either the child's or the parents', providing it is based on considerations of the best interests of the child."

The encroachment of this reinterpretation, the family court equivalent of "guilty until proven innocent," is one reason to support the Parental Rights Amendment. The amendment aims to provide protection for parents and their rights into the text of the US Constitution as follows:

- The liberty of parents to direct the upbringing, education, and care of their children is a fundamental right.
- The parental right to direct education includes the right to choose, as an alternative to public education, private, religious, or home schools, and the right to make reasonable choices within public schools for one's child.
- Neither the United States nor any State shall infringe these rights without demonstrating that its governmental interest as applied to the person is of the highest order and not otherwise served.
- The parental rights guaranteed by this article shall not be denied or abridged on account of disability.
- This article shall not be construed to apply to a parental action or decision that would end life.

Protecting children begins with the commonsense recognition that the vast majority of parents love and protect their children better than a judge or government agent can.

Chapter 2

What Is Parental Alienation?

"The supreme art of war is to subdue the enemy without fighting."

– Sun Tzu

Dr. Amy J. L. Baker, researcher, author or co-author of eight books, nationally and internationally recognized expert in parental alienation, and expert witness, provides a poignant definition of PA:

"Parental alienation is when one parent gives the children permission to break the other parent's heart."

This is indeed what happens when children turn against and completely reject a parent with whom they formerly had a loving and supportive relationship. Frequently, this parent is the one the children spend the most time with, and the alienator knows there is nothing in the world that would hurt that parent more than not having their children in their life. This is where the motivation in turning the children against them is born. In other words, the alienator's need to retaliate against the other parent, using their children as weapons, is more crucial to them than the well-being of their children.

When a parental relationship breaks down, the ideal scenario would involve two loving parents being concerned that their children suffer the least amount possible as a result of the divorce. Both parents behave as sane adults and arrange as close to 50/50 shared custody as possible. The children are not invited to participate and are not privy to the reasons their parents are splitting up, or the custody negotiations. These children grow up feeling secure, maintain their attachments to both parents and become mostly well-adjusted members of society.

At the other end of the spectrum is parental alienation. It most often occurs before, during, and after a high-conflict divorce, and there is no chance of amicable co-parenting occurring.

The alienation process usually begins when the children are young, so they are primed to reject the parent. The alienating parent will regularly make statements to the children like:

- "Your mother/father is always angry."
- "Your mother/father is taking drugs."
- "Don't pay any attention to him/her."

The denigration of the targeted parent can be subtle or overt. It is also progressive. It may come in the form of an alienating parent creating circumstances in which they can then sympathize with the child without ever saying anything negative about the other parent. Statements such as, "I'm so sorry you can't do/have X. I know how you feel." In response to situations they have created, for example, signing them up for an extracurricular activity without discussing it with the other parent, and it is on that parent's time with the child. Or unilaterally buying them a smartphone and then sympathizing with them when the other parent attempts to set some limits. The message is, "I am the nice parent and they are the mean parent." An alienated child reported that when her father picked them up, he would always have every child's favorite gum in the glove compartment and the most exciting activity planned for them. There were also no limits at his house, and the children did what they liked. After a while, he began making hostile and condemning remarks about their mother upon picking them up. Then his remarks became more abusive.

Eventually the children began to believe they could not love their mother and their mother did not love them. They believed their mother was abusive even though they had never seen any evidence of that. It was fabricated. The little girl described sitting at the dining table, slyly laughing at their mother, denigrating and being verbally abusive toward her. Their mother worked more than one job to meet the demands of the family and could not constantly "do fun things." It was not until the children were parents themselves, and this daughter was alienated from her own children, that they began to realize the injustice they had all suffered. Now, they have a close relationship with their mother and a distant relationship with their father.

In a separate case, a Wisconsin mother was accused of child abuse. There was an incident with her daughter (the daughter had injured the mother by slamming her hand in the door) but the police report that followed confirmed that there had been no instance of child abuse. However, the therapists believed the father's version, without interviewing the mom, and testified that there had been "a pattern of abuse." The Guardian Ad Litem (GAL) recommended the children be permanently removed from the mother. The father tried many times to file a restraining order against the mother, always unsuccessfully, and called the police often as a way of harassing her. The children were now describing their mother as abusive, whereas they previously said she was "loving and a good mother" and that they wished to have a relationship with both parents.

Despite the fact there was no evidence of abuse, the mother lost the ability to see her daughters, who would have "severe panic attacks" if they even saw a green van drive by that could have been their mother's. All the professionals declared them traumatized. The father sat passively in court and both the judge and GAL behaved as if they were the father's lawyers. They rejected outright all evidence that there was no abuse, and vehemently defended the father when he was described

10

as lying. This in spite of the fact the father had conducted an extra-marital affair for ten years, even fathering another child. He denied this in court and with therapists, and the judge asked the expert if it was justifiable that he lied. Because this judge abused the alienated mother for many years in court, he was finally recused from the case.

These situations are rampant throughout the world, and some will be described throughout this book. They are the most egregious cases, but the dynamics and treatment of the targeted parents by courts, schools, and communities are the same.

When the targeted parent leaves the relationship, the alienator's plan is usually already in place. What follows is the final brainwashing of the children, allowing less and less contact, and finally convincing people (the courts, family, schools, and friends) that the children do not want to see the targeted parent.

Getting the children to make false accusations against the parent, and to claim they do not want to be with the rejected parent concludes the whole Machiavellian process. Courts consider a child fourteen years and older to have reached the age to decide where they want to live. This action fails the child. Children are not allowed to drive, vote, drink, have sex with an adult, or travel without adult permission until they are aged sixteen, eighteen or twenty-one. How is a child of fourteen and even younger able to make the decision about which parent they want to live with, therefore rejecting the other parent? What damage does that do to the child?

Tragically, parental alienation is still largely misunderstood or even unknown by the vast majority of the population, which makes it difficult to identify when it is taking place. Dr. Richard Gardner, a pioneer in the study of Parental Alienation Syndrome (PAS), defined the following eight symptoms of alienation in children in his book *The International Handbook of Parental Alienation Syndrome: Conceptual, Clinical and Legal Considerations*:

1. A campaign of denigration of the alienated parent to family, friends, and whoever will listen. As Gardner explains "The denigration of the parent often has the quality of a litany. After only minimal prompting by a lawyer, judge, probation officer, mental health professional, or other person involved in the litigation, the record will be turned on and a command performance provided."

2. Weak, absurd, or frivolous rationalizations for the deprecation, and/or false accusation. For example, a sixteen-year-old claimed his father was not capable of taking care of him because he would not get up and get water for him during a movie they were watching. "Even years after the events have taken place, the child may justify the alienation with memories of minor altercations experienced in the relationship with the hated parent," Gardener says.

3. Lack of ambivalence in the child. Alienated children declare they do not want to see the alienated parent, period. There are no mixed feelings. This decision is not seen in

12

any other dynamic. (Even severely abused children want a relationship with an abusive parent.) A five-year old girl recently told me, "My mom is perfect and all-good. I love my mom. She never does anything wrong. My dad is bad all over. He's a mean person. I don't want to see my dad anymore."

4. Independent thinker phenomenon is present. The child says repeatedly that it is their decision alone to not see their parent, and they have not been persuaded by the alienator to cut off contact altogether. This is something I hear all the time. The child will maintain their alienating parent has nothing to do with their decision to not see their parent. It is totally their decisions. Adult children will say this too.

5. Reflexive support of the alienator no matter what. Alienated children insist the alienator is all good, and the alienated parent is the "bad" parent. Black and white, or split, thinking is present in alienation. The children will even refuse to accept obvious proof of the rejected parent's position. A child will defend the actions of their alienating parent, even by lying. No matter how gently or firmly the idea that the alienating parent misled them or lied to them, they will, with tears in their eyes, claim that parent is right and did not lie.

6. Absence of guilt for their actions and a complete disregard for the feelings of the discarded parent. There is a lack of gratitude for gifts, support payments, and other evidence of the rejected parent's continued love and involvement. One father reported when he took his youngest son gifts,

13

he would rip the card up without opening it, stomp on the balloons to pop them and said, "Stop wasting your money, I don't want anything from you." Another child pushed a senior dog off her bed, breaking her spine which resulted in her being put to sleep. She shows no remorse.

7. Borrowed scenarios are common. One often hears phraseology that is not commonly used by the child, but by the alienating parent. Many expressions are identical, and there is a rehearsed quality to their stories. A ten-year-old stood over his mother raising his voice and wagging his finger, saying she was still using drugs and the reason she did not test positive for the drug was because Meth only stays in your system for a few hours. His father who had custody of the boys, on the other hand, always tests positive for drugs because marijuana stays in the system for longer than 24 hours. Clearly, this was coming from the father. How would a child have that information, true or not.

8. Spread of animosity to the friends and/or extended family of the alienated parent. Children who have been removed from an abusive parent do not extend their rejection to extended family in the way alienated children do. Formerly loved grandparents, aunts, uncles, and cousins are viewed as equally dispensable as their hated parent.[2]

² Richard Gardner, S. Richard Sauber, and Demosthenes Lorandos, *The International Handbook of Parental Alienation Syndrome: Conceptual, Clinical and Legal Considerations* (Springfield: Charles C Thomas Publisher, 2006).

When his book was published in 2006, it was the most wide-ranging book available regarding parental alienation syndrome with contributions from thirty-one authors from eight countries around the world.

Although Dr. Gardner passed away in 2003, he continues to receive much undeserved, dishonest and unfair criticism, the likes of which remind us of the violence the alienator visits on their children, their former partners, and that partner's extended family. A similar situation occurred in the United Kingdom, where Dr. Ludwig Lowenstein was similarly attacked and dismissed vehemently by critics of parental alienation theory.

In 2020, Good Egg Safety CIC released a report on a year-long survey into the effects of parental alienation in the UK. Over 1500 parents impacted by alienation took part, and it was revealed that:

- more than half the respondents had not seen their children for more than 6 months
- 1 in 10 had not seen their child more than 5 years
- 58% have had custody arrangements breached multiple times
- 80% have suffered adverse health problems
- 55% have suffered serious financial impact
- 16 had completed or attempted suicide[3]

---

[3] Good Egg Safety CIC, "Parental Alienation Survey Research," 2020, London.

In a 2019 study, Jennifer Harman and her colleagues found that, "an estimated 1% of all children are alienated from a parental figure to some degree." As part of the study, a random digit dialing of home and cell phone numbers was conducted, with 13.4% of parents reporting they had at some point been a targeted parent, and about half of these stating the alienation was severe. From this information, they reached a generalized figure of more than 22 million adults who are impacted by PA.[4]

Being strategic and implementing a shared parenting plan before divorce is optimal. Because alienators are masters at finding loopholes in parenting plans, be sure to make one that is extremely specific, incredibly detailed, and always recorded in the court. Be clear about who picks up and who drops off. Define when a holiday stops and starts, including holiday weekends. Make it clear so there is no question about where the children are supposed to be on any given day. Also, include information about other parenting issues in your judgment. For example, consider adding that neither parent can schedule activities on the other parent's days. Do you want your child to have phone access to you on the other parent's days? If so, include it. Set the specific days and times the calls are made. How do you want medical appointments paid for? Do you split every bill and each pay the doctor/dentist separately? Who covers the children's

---

[4] Jennifer J. Harman, Sadie Leder-Elder, and Zeynep Biringen, "Prevalence of adults who are the targets of parental alienating behaviors and their impact," *Children and Youth Services Review* 106, (Nov 2019)

health insurance? Who claims the children on their tax return or do you alternate? The clearer you set everything up, the better for everyone involved.

The message here is, don't be naïve and imagine there will be no problems. Alienated parents frequently report that at first the sharing of child custody "is fine." However, if either of the parents become interested in someone else, problems can start and rapidly escalate. Be prepared to confront the anger of the alienating parent by having as close to an ironclad agreement as possible. This can prevent financial loss, emotional pain, and an endless lack of communication, which I will get into later.

I recently mediated a divorce where one partner did not wish to include anything about custody of their daughter. Both parents are lawyers, and the husband insisted they "would work it out" and their time and money should not be wasted discussing the issue. When I explained this could develop into a problem, he became irate. Fortunately, the wife could envision this potentially being an issue and insisted they agree on a custody arrangement and record how they would make adjustments in the future. Hopefully, this headed off any future custody conflicts.

It is common for alienated parents to be accused of abuse. To be clear, "abuse" does not include yelling at or smacking a child once, which often arises from the frustration the targeted parent feels due to the verbal and sometimes physical violence they endure at the hands of their deeply brainwashed children. Parents are only considered abusive when there is a *pattern* of abuse. The first step when a child accuses an adult of abuse is to talk to the other parent to find out what actually occurred. If abuse of any kind was happening, of course, it would not be considered alienation. Second, there are child abuse hotlines to call and social workers from the Department of Child and Family Services (DCFS) who will visit the child's house and investigate the situation. If there is serious abuse occurring and the situation is out of control, then the police should be called. They will determine the nature and seriousness of the abuse, then arrest the parent if the accusation has been substantiated. The police will then contact the Department of Child Protective Services (CPS) to determine whether the children would be safer if they were removed from the home.

All accusations of abuse should be thoroughly investigated. Where alienation is present, too often the police are called merely for the alienator to give false reports, and file exaggerated and untruthful charges against the targeted parent.

In one case, a young boy claimed to be sexually abused by his father. This false accusation resulted in a year-long investigation, and a report to the medical board against the father, almost resulting in him losing his medical license and livelihood. When questioned in reunification therapy about what happened, he said his father had touched his penis when he threw him in the swimming pool. This is NOT sexual abuse.

In a most recent case which is "being handled" by the Department of Child and Family Services, one son reported his father had digitally penetrated his anus one time. The father denies this. However, the case worker, minor's counsel, and other professionals involved believe it and do not allow the dad to be alone with his children. The mother does not show up for monitored visits and successfully portrays herself as a victim. After waiting two hours for her to arrive with the children for reunification therapy, calling her and sending messages, she left the following message a few hours later: "The boys are again strongly refusing to go to the therapy appointment. I am not able to get any of them into my car. I'm sorry. Warmly, SG." I have never met this mother, but the officials involved do not see anything amiss with this message. I explained I highly doubt the charges of sexual abuse and believe the mother is behind the false accusations. Their position is "children never lie about sexual abuse", while my position is children absolutely do lie, especially in alienation cases.

Another boy claimed his step grandfather abused him over Thanksgiving. Photos prove the grandfather was not there for the holiday, and there was no other history of the child being left alone with the grandfather. The grandfather did not have a history of pedophilia. Usually other children in the family are well aware of sexually abusive adults. There are many, many examples of these false accusations. They can, and do, destroy a parent's life.

How can this happen? The concept that the children have been brainwashed is frequently sneered at by the professional and lay community. However, the phenomenon of brainwashing has been well documented. Elizabeth Loftus, an author on the subject of mind control, and a distinguished researcher in the area of brainwashing, has conducted many studies in this area, including an experiment with college-age children. First she asked them if they had heard about something happening at the subway station that day. In a following class, she claimed some students had known about the incident. This was repeated daily. Eventually the whole class "knew about" the incident which never actually occurred. Her 2013 TED talk (which can be seen on YouTube) raises many questions on the reliability of memories and provides an interesting overview of her studies and findings.[5]

Most people know about the events that took place in the South American country of Guyana in 1978. Jim Jones moved a large number of people there from the US, and named the town after himself—Jonestown. The "town" was a polite word for a cult and he was their leader and under investigation by the US government at the request of the concerned families in the United States. Upon the team of investigators arriving at Jonestown, Jones persuaded his followers to drink cyanide laced Kool-Aid, killing 900 people, including children. (Hence the term "Drinking the Kool-Aid" which means believing false information given by an individual.) Parents gave the poison to their children

---

[5] Elizabeth Loftus, "How reliable is your memory?" filmed September 2013 at TEDGlobal, Edinburgh, Scotland, video, 17:24, https://www.ted.com/talks/elizabeth_loftus_how_reliable_is_your_memory.

first. Jones himself had his nurse shoot him and then herself. How could so many people have been persuaded to kill their children and then themselves? Undoubtedly this was the result of brainwashing.

Alienators will go to any lengths to destroy a child's relationship with a beloved parent, to punish that parent for leaving them. They are usually narcissistic, sometimes sociopathic, often psychotic, and invariably grandiose. They view both the other parent and their children as possessions to be done with as they wish, without regard to the law. In other words, they do not follow court orders, custody agreements, requests for mediation, agreements reached in mediation, and will lie indiscriminately. Their intention is to destroy the bond between the parent and child without regard to their child's welfare.

Some alienated children have shared with me how, in the absence of their alienated parent they take care of their alienator parent. When the marriage ends, many alienators burden the child with the caretaking chores like washing the family's clothes, cooking meals, cleaning the house, and more. They essentially take over the role of the rejected parent. The alienating parent will become irate if the chores are not completed. Adult children say they took care of their alienator parent, and feel obligated to do so because that parent is the victim, by having them stay with them after the divorce. This meant they had no time for a partner, and most often spent their free time "socializing" with their parent.

In my work, I have mostly dealt with alienating parents who are narcissists, but the diagnoses of sociopath is also prevalent. Narcissism is on a continuum of personality disorders. The scale includes borderline personality disorder, narcissistic personality disorder, sociopathic disorder and psychotic disorder, the latter being the most severe. Alienators are most often considered to be narcissists and are themselves victims of narcissistic abuse as children. Their grandiosity defines them. Those displaying a sociopathic disorder are frequently involved in criminal activity, and may have been to jail. They are similar to narcissists in that they are charming, cool, calm, and collected. Both these personality disorders are rarely, if ever, seen participating in psychotherapy. They believe they are beyond reproach and "don't need therapy." They will say "the therapist said I was fine, and I don't need to be in therapy." When an alienator does go to therapy and enjoys it, it is likely they have found a similar narcissist as a therapist, who has validated and complimented them, despite the need for the existing problems to be brought to light. In the same way some celebrities will deliberately seek out a therapist who is so impressed they are seeing someone famous that they agree with everything their client says, the alienator will often handpick a therapist who does the same.

Narcissists will allow their children to live with them forever and in fact encourage their dependence. Narcissists are codependent and will make their children their playmates. Uninformed bystanders will consider them to be "good with children" and admire them when they socialize with the children instead of the adults.

Narcissists first idealize but then abruptly begin to devalue and eventually abuse their partner in the relationship. Perhaps this devaluation and annihilation is what children are unconsciously aware of and wish to avoid. The narcissist's employment of lies, insults, condescension, derision, and false allegations are all forms of abuse. It is a mistake to imagine they do not behave in the same manner to their children, despite the fact that the children vehemently defend the alienator and deny they are mistreated by them. For an insight into narcissistic behavior, the YouTube videos of author, and self-proclaimed narcissist Sam Vaknin, offer a detailed explanation.

Borderline personality disorders are characterized by instability and fluctuation of moods. Their dependence on others and fear of being abandoned are the reason this diagnosis is sometimes applied to the alienator, however, the narcissistic personality disorder is diagnosed more frequently. The borderline personality disorder initially presents as "together", charming, and believable, but dissolves fairly easily when challenged and exposed.

Psychotic individuals have no feelings and do not care about other's feelings. They can also be charming initially. While there are key differences in these disorders, one thing they all have in common is that they can be abusive, violent, and dangerous.

The children are the abuser's greatest source of leverage over their ex-partner. Narcissists will discredit the alienated parent by using vicious rumors and charging him/her with offences they have not committed. They will use others to stalk, harass and threaten the rejected parent, and include the children in these activities. Children are used to spy, hack computers and phones, go through a parent's personal belongings, and even steal. They then dutifully report back to the alienator, who uses the newly gleaned information to further the case against the targeted parent.

Children learn subliminally that the narcissistic parent gets what they want from bullying, lying, stealing, and pushing others' boundaries. The alienator shows the children the other parent is "weak", and urges them to hurt the other parent by behaving in a malicious manner toward him or her. There could be nothing more hurtful to a parent than complete rejection by their children. The child will then align themselves with the alienator to protect themselves from similar aggression.

Children desire relationships with their parents. Notably, children will seek out parents who gave them up for adoption, or even those who abused them. This is merely to describe how forgiving children are and how much they desire a relationship with their missing parent. In their book *Bonded to the Abuser*, Amy J. L. Baker, Ph.D. and Mel Schneiderman, Ph.D. describe how children who are abused will want a relationship with the abusing parent and even become protective and defensive of that parent despite the pain they are causing.[6]

---

[6] Amy J.L. Baker, and Mel Schneiderman, Bonded to the Abuser, (Lanham: Rowman & Littlefield, 2015).

More often than not, parents who are alienated describe the close relationships they had with their children before the rejection took place. They have letters, cards, videos, and other materials to prove the attachment, and how loving the child was to them and vice versa. One mother commented how strangers, family and friends, would reference how loving she and her daughters were to each other. They have now been alienated for ten years.

Alienated children have been manipulated into believing they should reject a parent they love in order to maintain favor with the alienating parent. The court, social workers, GALs, evaluators, and therapists repeatedly misunderstand the situation and dismiss that PA is happening at all. In this sense, they are manipulated themselves, failing the children in the process. The best interest of all children includes having both loving parents in their lives, unless one parent is abusive. Again, keep in mind, one episode of a parent losing control and grabbing the child is NOT abuse.

Alienating parents seek revenge on their ex-spouse more intensely than they love their children. A savvy judge once ordered an alienating parent to write one thousand times "From now on, I will love my children more than I hate my ex." An alienator said she would show her ex how expensive it would be to divorce her and that he would never see his children again. Despite the fact this was in a court document, minor's counsel and DCFS insist there is no alienation present and she is "just a mom trying to protect her children." At this time, the children are "too afraid of their father to be in the same room as him." They were never afraid of him before the divorce began.

Chapter 3

How Does It Happen?

"The peak efficiency of knowledge and strategy is
to make conflict unnecessary."

– Sun Tzu

*P*arental alienation occurs when the child rejects a parent,
and chooses not to see them. But how does this even
begin to happen?

The term "Stockholm syndrome" originated from an
attempted bank robbery that took place in Stockholm,
Sweden in 1973. Customers were taken as hostages, and while
captive, developed sympathetic feelings for the robber. The
bond they formed endured even after their release, when
they went on to testify in court on his behalf.

The cognitive dissonance that is created in a situation where adults and children are taken hostage and required to come to terms with a dangerous situation, can resolve with them identifying with the abuser/oppressor. It is a tactic employed to save themselves. In the case of parental alienation, children who witness what can happen to a targeted member of the family, accordingly change their reality to match that of the alienator. They do this to survive, and to maintain the love and approval of the alienating parent.

Alienators will also make staying with them enticing. Children are excused from school, plied with material objects, not forced to attend therapy, and promised monitory support. It is also (on the surface) an easier situation because they do not have to answer to the parent whom they have rejected and lied about. They do not have to bear witness to the devastation and grief the targeted parent is experiencing. It becomes the path of least resistance, and their minds are altered, sometimes forever.

An alienator will often go to extreme lengths to punish the targeted parent, and without intervention, this can lead to tragedy. A real and terrible example of this, is the case of Michele Neurauter, a mother of three girls, who was a victim of parental alienation for many years. In 2017, she was murdered by her ex-husband, with the help of her middle daughter, Karrie, who was nineteen years old at the time.

By all accounts, Michele was a loving mother. Her ex-husband, Lloyd, had a long history of physical abuse towards her (police reports were filed twenty-six times), and she had stayed at shelters with the children several times to escape the abuse. Lloyd was described as a strict disciplinarian, who was observed to be abusive towards his daughters as well. He left his wife and daughters to take a job elsewhere, and the couple divorced and he remarried. He filed for custody of the children when he was court ordered to pay child support. His strategy of alienation included making false accusations to authorities and to his daughters against their mother.

Michele documented the alienation of the children for many years before she was murdered.

Immediately before the murder, Lloyd confided in his daughters that he could not pay child support and didn't know what to do, other than commit suicide, which probably frightened them. As an alternative, Lloyd proposed killing Michele. He persuaded Karrie to assist him and they planned the murder a week ahead of time.

When Lloyd strangled Michele, Karrie helped him stage it to look like a suicide by hanging her from the stair banister. The youngest daughter was in the house at the time, and when they left, they took her with them. The investigators suspected Lloyd and Karrie and tapped their phones. In one sinister call, Lloyd can be heard telling Karrie to pretend to cry about her mother's death.

The first thing Lloyd did when he was called about Michele's death was to cancel child support and try to claim Michele's life insurance. After three months of investigation, the police moved to arrest Lloyd and Karrie. When they found Lloyd, he threatened suicide by jumping off a parking structure. Lloyd was charged with first degree murder and Karrie with second degree murder. Before the trial, Lloyd insinuated Karrie was solely responsible for murdering her mother. When this failed, he then claimed to have killed Michele because he was afraid she would abuse the children, before eventually pleading guilty to first-degree murder.

The District Attorney commented that parental alienation had existed in this family for many years, and was well documented by Michele. He insightfully articulated that the aim of an alienating parent is the "complete devaluation" of the alienated parent. It is this annihilation that "justifies" in the mind of an alienator and the alienated children the psychological and, in this instance, the physical killing of a parent.

Lloyd is now serving a life sentence without parole. Karrie was convicted of second-degree manslaughter, and after serving a short sentence, has now been released from jail. The oldest and youngest daughters are still convinced Michele "deserved" to be murdered. A frightening prospect indeed.

Unfortunately, this tragedy is not an isolated incident. Parents kill their children to prevent the other parent from gaining custody and an ex-spouse is killed too, as "punishment."

We would like to believe that Michele's death was not in vain. Perhaps this tragedy will help bring awareness to the issue of parental alienation.

Parental alienation has been observed to progress through three distinct stages: mild, moderate and severe.

1) Mild – In the initial stage, targeted parents may notice changes in the child such as:

- The child displays odd behavior upon arriving from the alienator's home.
- A refusal to return to the alienating parent's home develops. The child becomes anxious, tearful, angry, or upset at the prospect of being with the alienator because of the comments against the targeted parent.
- The child begins to criticize the targeted parent, their home, and other members of their formerly adored family.
- The words the child uses are adult expressions, and are used by the other parent.
- The child wants to contact the other parent during visits.
- The child displays unexplained stress and/or anxiety.

2) Moderate – At this stage, symptoms have escalated and may include:

- The child makes excuses and does not want to go to the targeted parent's home.
- The child becomes rude and angry and refuses to accept the targeted parent's authority.

- The targeted parent begins to feel afraid of the child, their temper tantrums, and physical abuse.
- The child begins to reject the targeted parent's extended family.
- They begin to lie about the targeted parent.
- The other parent over-empowers the child, allowing them to make decisions about school, therapy, and custody.

3) Severe – In the end, the targeted parent is rejected by their child in the following ways:

- The child refuses to visit or see the targeted parent.
- The child is aligned with the other parent; defends the other parent.
- They refuse to discuss the rejection of the targeted parent with the parent or anyone else.
- They "act" as if they are terrified of the targeted parent. This can be quite dramatic.
- They have become empowered by the alienator and will not accept authority from the targeted parent.

If viewed and commented on by an unacquainted bystander, they will opine that, "Something must have occurred to make the child reject that parent." Of course, in some cases this is true, and there truly is abuse by the estranged parent. However, in an alienation case, the child rejects the parent for no substantial reason. "You brag too much", "I don't like the way you talk", "You sign me up for extracurricular activities without consulting me", "You make me put my money in the bank" or they just repeat the lies they have heard from the other parent. A ten-year-old boy told me his mother was trying to get full custody of him. Of course he had no idea what he was talking about, and the mother was not doing any such thing.

You'll often hear the terms "targeted parent", "rejected parent", and "alienated parent" used interchangeably, but they each have their own distinct meanings.

The **targeted parent** is a victim of PA in the early stages, and is currently still in a position to see their child.

The **rejected parent** is experiencing negative behavior from their child that is becoming more intense and impacting the level of contact.

The **alienated parent** is now in a situation where there is no longer contact between the parent and child.

Chapter 4

The Alienator,
Alienated Parent,
And Child

"If you know your enemy and you know yourself,
you need not fear the results of a hundred battles."
– Sun Tzu

*W*hether you are a target of alienation yourself, a concerned family member watching on, or a professional involved in the case, understanding the three parties at the center of PA is essential.

THE ALIENATOR

While parental alienators are not yet widely talked about, it appears at least some of the techniques they employ are common practice in divorced families. In 2013, the American Bar Association published a book titled *Children Held Hostage: Identifying Brainwashed Children, Presenting a Case and Crafting Solutions*, in which authors Stanley Clawar and Brynne Rivlin shared the findings from a study of over 1000 families affected by PA. The results showed that 86 percent of divorcing parents admitted to brainwashing their children against the other parent at least once a week, and 23 percent said they did it once a day. However, alienators will deny they ever bad mouth the other parent, and children will back them up—but when children are frequently using adult words they have no understanding of, it indicates they are parroting what the alienator has said.[7]

The alienating parent thrives on conflict, refusing to follow court orders, and ignoring restraining orders. In their own peculiarly deluded, self-aggrandized way, they exert their authority over the school, their children, the targeted parent, extended family, psychotherapists, and various officers of the court. Alienating parents can be ultimately charming and impressive in front of others and especially with custody evaluators, judges, and others who may help them get what they want. Professionals will often side with them in their ignorance of the counterintuitive nature of parental alienation.

---

[7] Stanley S. Clawar, and Brynne V. Rivlin, *Children Held Hostage: Identifying Brainwashed Children, Presenting a Case and Crafting Solutions*, (Chicago: American Bar Association, 2013).

In a situation I am presently involved in, the alienating father is abusive to almost anyone involved with his daughter. The orthodontist, who had been told horror stories about the girl's mother by the father, was surprised to hear the mother wanted to pay for her daughter's braces and that she was pleasant and cooperative. As soon as the payment plan was set up, the father insisted on paying half. He then demanded the mother pay for a tutor for the daughter, and when one was found, he demanded not one but three names, and *he* would choose which one. He constantly counter-parents no matter what the situation is. The intention he has is to stay in complete control, no matter how it affects his daughter. He sabotages any visitation with the mother, and has his daughter call his girlfriend "mom." He makes scenes at graduations, and prevents phone calls. We have proposed to the judge that he be sanctioned and further sanctioned with fines and even loss of custody should he continue to sabotage any relationship with the mother and extended family.

Another case I'm currently involved in also happens to have an alienating father who goes out of his way to block contact between the mother and their ten-year-old daughter. This alienator has their daughter telephone her mom, insult her mom, and then hang up. The father then texts the mother and says, "Look what you did. You're ruining your relationship with her. It's no one's fault but your own." He would not allow their daughter to attend school events if her mom was going to be there. He kept her from school if he knew mom was volunteering that day. He coached her to say negative things about her mom to the therapist. This ten-year-old was so stressed, she had a panic attack and said she wanted to kill herself.

This is an alienator who was determined by a judge to be alienating his other children in a previous marriage.

Parental alienation does not support the old-fashioned Family Systems point of view. This is not the 50/50 responsibility of a dissolving marriage in the Family Systems Theory. Linda Gottlieb, LMFT, LCSW-R, author, expert witness and reconciliation therapist, proposes it is more like 90/10, with the alienators causing 90 percent of the conflict and alienation of the children. For more information on this and other aspects of PA, visit the End Parental Alienation website (www.EndParentalAlienation. com) where Linda has collated a wide range of educational resources.

Alienators will keep the targeted parent battling in court for an extended period of time, until they are financially and psychologically exhausted. Imagine the helplessness of the targeted parent, who has not done any of what they have been accused of, being forced to deny the false accusations and charges. The accusation always sounds stronger than the denial. The preponderance of evidence for these false accusations should be on the alienator, but instead, targeted parents have to fight for their right to see their children and to be involved in their children's lives, while simultaneously fending off these malicious accusations. Unfortunately, most targeted parents are frequently unsuccessful.

The alienator will not cease with this persecution until he/she wins primary custody of their children. Even if they do not win the custody, they work very hard at getting the children to hate the targeted parent and refuse to visit the parent in spite of court orders.

However, we are starting to see a shift and more hope in court cases. In a situation I have direct knowledge of, the parents appeared in court 128 times in eleven years, finally resulting in the judge stripping the alienator of 100 percent legal and physical custody, only allowing the alienator monitored visits every other Saturday, never to exceed eight hours. Once the alienator lost custody, he stopped exercising his visitation entirely. The child is now thriving, happy and has returned to having a great relationship with his mother, who he was previously alienated from for a solid year. This mother had an arduous journey, but she didn't give up and she prevailed. You can too.

In the book *Surviving Parental Alienation*, Dr. Amy J. L. Baker and Paul R. Fine identified the following techniques that are frequently used by the alienating parent:

- Badmouthing the targeted parent and their family
- Limiting the children's contact with that parent
- Withdrawing love/getting angry with the child
- Telling the children the other parent does not love them
- Telling the children the parent abused and abandoned them
- Confiding in the child about their version of the adult relationship

- Forcing a child to choose loyalty
- Creating the impression the other parent is dangerous
- Limiting photos and contact with the extended family
- Forcing a child to reject the other parent
- Belittling the other parent in front of the child
- Creating conflict between the parent and child
- Cultivating dependency on the alienating parent
- Interrogating the child after visitations
- Making the child feel guilty about a positive relationship with the targeted parent
- Having the child spy on the other parent
- Having the child refer to someone else as mom/dad and the targeted parent by their first name
- Calling the child insistently while they are with the other parent
- Telling the child to call them while with the other parent
- Asking the child to record the other parent while on the phone
- Listening in on calls with the other parent
- Hanging up when the other parent calls and encouraging the child to do so too[8]

We can add reading to the children carefully selected sections of court papers that are known to be false. Just today a ten-year-old yelled at his mother that she wanted "sole physical and legal custody" and that she had no right to want that. He (the boy) was demanding he make the decision, not her.

---

[8] Amy J.L. Baker, and Paul R. Fine, *Surviving Parental Alienation*, (Lanham: Rowman & Littlefield, 2017).

The mother has 75 percent physical custody and 50 percent legal. Alienators also have children read conversations on communication apps like Talking Parents or Our Family Wizard which are intended to be private.

One way to identify if the child has been subjected to these manipulations is if they parrot the language they have heard from the alienator (as in the above example) at home or in court. For example, a five-year-old might say, "You never commit yourself to anything!" They are taught to relegate the targeted parent's role to nothing of importance in their life.

Consequences in the child of this kind of manipulation is depression, feelings of worthlessness, substance abuse, lack of trust, low academic performance, low career performance, and suicide. The child eventually feels tremendous guilt and shame for treating their rejected parent so poorly and abusively. This guilt and shame is very difficult for them to live with once they understand alienation and how it exists in their family. When the enormity of the situation dawns on them, they often reject the alienating parent, or keep a distance from them. A young woman, formerly alienated from her father, stated:

> "My dad always said my mom raised me to hate him. But my mom raised me to hate myself, and he's just part of me." She went on to say, "I hate myself for how I treated him."

An alienated parent can help their child when they hear these kinds of statements. They can reassure their child they understand why they said those things and they want to move forward and have a relationship with them. As adults, attending psychotherapy would be helpful. Again, choosing a therapist who is knowledgeable about alienation is important, or they may tend to dismiss what the child did and not deal with their guilt and shame.

To the parent with a personality disorder, the rejection of them is a replay of their own rejection as a child. They cannot see how they abused, and do not like that view of themselves, and will become the narcissistic parent who abused them. They do not see themselves as dysfunctional or monstrous, but rather as great, a gem, unique, irresistible. Many will take on the characteristics of the partner and present themselves that way. For example, they are now the animal lover, the patient one, the one who loves to cook, the non-violent, never angry partner. They present themselves that way, and that is why they are able to charm and convince all around them who are unable to see who they really are. They are unable to see who they are and if they catch a glimpse, they decompensate and can be violent, psychotic, and above all, alienators.

Their goal is to destroy and humiliate the abandoning partner. Their objective is to reestablish their power, control, and mastery over the former spouse. They will prey on the partner's vulnerabilities to render them powerless. They do not care about anything but revenge, and if their children are victims to this, so be it.

Alienators require idealized worship from their children, and provide conditional love. **Children cannot separate from**

them and are discarded when they push the narcissist off their pedestal. When it happens to young children it is devastating. It causes a lack of empathy and dysfunction in the alienated child/adult. They may come to enjoy inflicting pain on people, including the rejected parent. "Grooming" of the child takes place by the alienating parent, and the targeted parent can be negated into non-existence.

THE ALIENATED PARENT

If you think about soldiers returning from war, some are traumatized and do not appear to resemble who they were before they went to war. They suffer from anxiety attacks, nightmares, physical illness, depression, anger, suicidal ideation, and much more. They suffer from post-traumatic stress disorder.

This is what the alienated parent experiences as well. They suffer from all the above and much more. At times, they are "unable to keep it together." They may "lose it," and react with rage at the sheer injustice of the situation they are experiencing because it is so incomprehensible to them. They may become disorganized and repeat themselves, desperately wanting someone to listen and acknowledge their pain, persecution, and desperation. Most importantly, they need others to believe them. After all, alienation is so inhumane and cruel, it's difficult to believe any parent would abuse their child by alienating them and filling their minds with falsehoods about the alienated parent.

Clinicians and the courts alike, tend to perceive the manifestations of this trauma suffered by the alienated parent as nothing more than a personality disorder. They mistakenly attribute the manifested symptoms to a character disorder in the parent who is collapsing emotionally. The alienated parent is prone to being misdiagnosed and deemed pathological. Manifestation of the trauma (anger, fear, emotional lability, suicidal ideation, and/or attempted suicide) is viewed as a personality **trait** as opposed to a transient **state** of a stress/trauma reaction. This is known as a "fundamental attribution error" perpetrated by clinicians, lawyers, court personal and DCFS caseworkers, who are not trained or educated to diagnose in parental alienation situations. The reactions of alienated parents are in response to the trauma of rejection, humiliation, and maltreatment at the hands of their beloved children. This is an **appropriate** way to respond to losing access to one's children, family, and friends with no understanding why and when there is no justice forthcoming.

Alienated parents are described as having traits of borderline personality disorder which is ironic since that is one of the chief personality disorders suffered by the alienating parent, lethally combined with narcissistic personality disorder. To clarify, **traits** actually describe the overall functioning in one's life. Thus a parent who maintains their career, pays for their child's needs, does not commit crimes, has those **traits.** On the other hand, a **state** has to do with a recent traumatic event that has caused psychosis, depression, hysteria, anger, and suicidal ideation. A parent in such a state of trauma cannot be diagnosed as having a personality disorder unless there is a **pattern** of this type of behavior, self-reported or personally observed by a therapist, and not relayed by an alienated child or alienating parent to the courts, DCFS, or an expert witness. An alienated parent may be experiencing post-traumatic stress disorder, but this should only be diagnosed by a suitably qualified professional. Therapists, evaluators and "experts" who lack training in PA will frequently diagnose an alienated parent with borderline personality disorder, sometimes without having even met them! This is highly unethical, and the therapist can be reported to their licensing boards for diagnosing an individual whom they are not treating.

I have witnessed alienated children coming into therapy, asserting their "boundaries" and "right" to treat their alienated parents abusively. For example, they "set boundaries" by not allowing texts, messages, gifts, or visits. Their response when challenged is, "that is my right" to (for example) "deny him/her an invitation to graduation" or to "step foot on my school grounds" etc. In traditional psychotherapy, the therapist thinks they have "helped" that child to "assert their needs." Later, the alienated child, now an adult, becomes irate when a therapist refuses to "validate her feelings" like her original therapist did in the past. In reality, therapists who assume they are helping the children are actually supporting and repeating the alienator's behavior. The trained therapist will challenge these assertions, ask what the alienated parent did to deserve such rejection and not allow the child to get away with platitudes. Children become quite tearful and remorseful when these defenses are eliminated and reconciliation occurs quickly after that hurdle is overcome.

When a parent loses a child to death, they are afforded great sympathy and support. But when a child is lost through alienation, that parent is misunderstood and judged in the most egregious fashion imaginable, and not allowed to grieve, or rage. A friend of mine who tragically is an alienated mom that has also experienced the death of her child, says the suffering of being an alienated parent is in many ways worse than having a child die, as there can be closure in death, but not in alienation.

THE ALIENATED CHILD

"Splitting" is a defense mechanism, and in the case of alienated children, they see the targeted parent as all bad, and the alienator as all good. Children who are alienated against a parent often employ this tactic as a result of the intolerable and relentless emotional pressure to hate the alienated parent, which is inflicted upon them by the alienating parent. It is an immature defense, causing polarized views of themselves and others to develop. Seeing the alienated parent as "all bad," and the alienator as "all good" is their way of coping with an irresolvable situation. It is this polarization that causes their lack of ambivalence and devaluation of the alienated parent, to the point that the parent no longer matters to them.

In their minds, the problem is the alienated parent. It is *always* his or her fault. *Everything* they do is terrible, and there is no room for human error. The blaming is relentless. Making mistakes and asking for forgiveness is not possible, whereas the favored parent can do no wrong, and is almost perfect. Children will tell me, with regard to the targeted parent, that their parent has "forfeited" the right to be their parent based on a frivolous complaint, such as, "They (therapist and mother) made me cry in therapy."

A sixteen-year-old recently told me he couldn't stand his alienated father because his dad "thought he was so great." Upon inquiring what he meant, he said his father was the first in his family to graduate from college! I challenged this and asked why he wasn't proud of his dad for his achievement. He looked somewhat shame-faced when confronted and claimed his father "bragged" about having a college degree. He himself wanted to go to college, but demeaned his father for doing just that. It was after this session that he finally saw the reality of the situation and changed 180 degrees. He even consented to going on a long vacation with his dad, his dad's new partner, and cousins adopted by his father. He reported they "had an awesome time" and was on his way to spend the weekend with his father and the family again. An amazing change indeed.

To the targeted parent's disbelief, the children claim the other parent was always present and provided everything that was positive to them while they were being raised. They claim not to remember one joyous experience with the alienated parent. Even when presented with evidence to the contrary, they claim they just pretended they enjoyed the experience.

This type of polarization does not bode well for the child as it is carried into the adult relationships. One person is right, the other wrong. They love the other or they hate the other.

There is no middle ground. All evidence received goes into one container. The other person is "always angry", "always taking pills", "never wants to do what I want to do", "always wants their way", etc.

A child has to be taught to hate a once much-loved parent. It does not come naturally nor is there a logical progression leading inexorably to hate. Their love for their devoted parent, which was previously unconditional, is willfully, maliciously, and systematically destroyed by their alienating parent. Teenagers and older children can be persuaded easily to hate their parent whereas younger children have to be persuaded and bribed. Even adult children, who were not alienated as children, can come to hate their beloved parent. They believe the alienator is confiding in them, when in reality the alienator is lying. History is constantly being rewritten by the alienator. Those lies, when repeated often enough, even in the face of scant evidence, become irrefutable facts. For example, if a child is told repeatedly that their other parent abuses drugs, or is "always angry", they will come to believe it and believe that is also their own experience with the alienated parent.

The alienation and distancing can take place for many years before the parents separate, so that by the time of the divorce, the child has already begun to believe falsehoods about the targeted parent. If the child continues to have a relationship with the targeted parent, or if there is reunification therapy, the negative view of the target parent does not continue. A child can get their own perspective on both parents and adapt to having both parents in their life.

The alienator forms what is called in Family Systems Theory "The Perverse Triangle." They form a coalition with their child against the rejected parent. The children either reject the alienated parent, thereby aligning themselves, unwillingly at first, with the alienator, or they incur the wrath of that parent. By rejecting the targeted parent, they are actually rejecting themselves because they are also part (half) of the rejected parent. Dr. Amy J. L. Baker states that the alienators make their assertions "so real to the child that the child loses the reality of (their) own feelings."

For example, in one of my sessions, a pre-teen boy stood over his mother, yelling at her and behaving exactly like his father. The boy accused her of continuing to use drugs and going to a bogus drug treatment facility. The treatment facility's director was telephoned in the session, and she reminded the boys they had both been at the facility and it was not bogus. She remembered their mother and confirmed the mother had indeed graduated from the facility. The director also remembered the mom's concern about her sons possibly being alienated when she was in the treatment facility. This mom's instincts were correct. The boys claimed to have seen court documents informing them the facility was bogus. The director handled it well, both reminding them and confronting them with the facts. Finally, the boys agreed to put this accusation behind them and work on their relationship with their mother, and the remainder of the session went well. However, when the boys returned to their dad that evening, they reverted to claiming they had been lied to by their mother.

This behavior is not unique; it is standard for alienated children.

Returning to the alienator is of course the problem. Whatever progress is made during the therapy is promptly destroyed because the children know the alienator does not want to hear good things about the targeted parent. In this scenario, the boys became more abusive to their mother, one even refusing to see her the following session.

Unfortunately, social workers, judges, GALs, and other professionals involved, believe that weekly reconciliation therapy is a viable option. It is most definitely not. Returning to the alienator is a disaster unless there is some built-in sanction from the judge preventing the alienator from further sabotaging any reconciliation with the other parent.

Chapter 5

Getting Ready For War

"All war is deception."

– Sun Tzu

*M*ost parents who begin to realize they are losing their children as a result of being alienated by the other parent, extended family and others, are typically unprepared and initially refuse to accept the gravity of what is taking place. They are not yet acquainted with the concept of alienation as it relates to them and their children and how horrific the consequences of their lack of knowledge will be.

Alienation usually begins from within the marriage or relationship, escalates through the divorce and becomes lethal as the targeted parent begins to understand the enormity of their loss. They go through many stages of disbelief, anger and grief. It is the worst devastation that can ever be committed against a parent. The alienation is referred to as "The Living Death." The children may be down the block, or in the same town, but absent from their life. The lack of any contact with their children, reinforced by their own children who are psychologically coerced into parroting the alienating parent's hatred of the targeted parent, is gut-wrenching. The searing pain of watching their children recede from the formerly loving relationship can be unbearable. The lack of closure when they realize they will most likely not see or hear from their children again for months, years, or maybe for the rest of their lives, and never fully comprehending the intensity of the alienating parent's desire to psychologically, physically, and financially destroy them, can shatter a parent.

When alienated parents go to court, they, and frequently their lawyers, are unprepared for the hostility with which they are met, the attacks made on their character, the false accusations of drug use, abuse, neglect, infidelity, and more. The targeted parent's disorganization from their rage at how unfair and unjust their newfound situation has become, makes them look like the parent at fault in the minds of the lawyers and the judge. This impression of them as fragmented and unstable will remain over time. Research shows negative impressions upon meeting someone for the first time generally endures despite the positive experience that may follow. That negative impression will survive for the duration of the court experience.

The alienated parents are inevitably blindsided by the false accusations. The alienator is ready with the deception they have planned, putting the alienated parent on the defensive, while they sit smugly supported by various entities to whom they have revealed the "truth" about the targeted parent. He or she is unprepared for the violence that has been unleashed against them. They flail around, not knowing how to respond, but invariably "lose it" and react with their own rage and frustration.

This disorganization causes the targeted parent to repeat themselves, wanting and needing someone to listen and to believe them, to acknowledge their pain, their persecution and desperation. When a targeted parent realizes they are being alienated from their children, the shock is profound. These parents relate that they experience feelings close to what can be described as psychosis. Their world is unrecognizable. The unreality of the situation rocks their psyche. Nothing seems real. Emotions are uncontrollable. Can they have really lost their child/children? Is the other parent really causing this situation? Parents report feelings of disbelief that the former spouse could be capable of such abuse and cruelty. They question repeatedly what they did wrong to deserve this treatment. Did they actually abuse their children? Why is the ex-spouse treating them this way? The ex-spouse knows how much the alienated parent loves their children.

The answer is at once complicated and simple:

The alienating parent believes that the children and the other parent are their possessions. They are humiliated at being rejected and abandoned and will go to any length to take revenge against the other parent.

The example of Lloyd Neurater, who murdered the mother of his children and brainwashed their daughter Karrie to participate in the killing of her mother, is an example of what can happen when parental alienation is permitted to progress. Lloyd was the one who left the marriage and had remarried. He knew his ex-wife was happier without him and she was determined not to give up her fight for custody of their children. When she filed for child support, he intensified his alienation of the children against her and with his daughter, developed a plan to kill her. He was not going to allow her to have his money and his children.

These are the workings of a mind suffering from a combination of personality disorders, such as narcissism, sociopathy, and psychosis.

BEYOND GRIEF

Targeted parents are vilified. As Amy J. L. Baker, Ph.D., and Paul R. Fine, P.R. describe in their book *Surviving Parental Alienation: A Journey of Hope and Healing*, there are five primary manipulation techniques used by the alienator to facilitate the campaign of denigration:

1. Expressing persistent and merciless denigration of the target parent's character in order to minimize his/her importance.

2. Creating the notion that the target parent is detrimental to the child and must be feared.

3. Questioning the target parent's love for their child in order to destroy the psychological bond between the child and the target parent.

4. Withdrawal of love by the alienating parent from a child who acknowledges positive feelings and regard for the target parent.

5. Obliterating the target parent from the emotional and physical life of the child.[9]

Added to the false accusations, the alienator encourages the children to carry a campaign of hate into the targeted parent's home. This creates a combustible situation with the targeted parent trying to make sense of what is happening. The children are made to file false accusations which involve the various "protective" agencies in their lives. These accusations are also made to family and friends. This is an impossible situation. The parent is guilty because the alienator says so, and when backed up by the children, it is a fait accompli, or a done deal. Nothing sounds weaker than claiming "I didn't do that" over and over again.

The reaction of the targeted parent to this overwhelming tsunami in their lives is similar, if not identical, to Elizabeth Kubler Ross's five stages of grief:

---

[9] Amy J.L. Baker, and Paul R. Fine, *Surviving Parental Alienation: A Journey of Hope and Healing*, (Lanham: Rowman & Littlefield, 2017).

- denial
- anger
- bargaining
- depression
- acceptance

The parent finds themselves cycling through the first four stages of grief. Acceptance, if and when it ever comes, arrives painfully, slowly. At first, in denial, they cannot believe what is happening to them or the extent of the denigration. The sense of betrayal they feel at the hands of the alienating parent, formerly their lover and best friend, their family, friends, and even their own children is devastating. The realization of the enormity of the situation, to be cut out of their children's lives, is unbearable.

Anger rises together with the helplessness the targeted parent experiences in the situation. They are suddenly thrust into the legal arena and forced to find funds for lawyers who may very well be ignorant about the counterintuitive nature of parent alienation.

Bargaining occurs when the targeted parent tries to appeal to their former spouse, their children and former friends. The majority of the helping profession offers no comfort and uses the old model of sharing the blame and believing the children. Going to a therapist who knows nothing about alienation is usually more detrimental than not going to a therapist at all.

The depression and isolation the targeted parent experiences is excruciating. They have lost their children. Some targeted parents commit suicide. It happens when the parent feels hopeless, helpless, and alone. They are unable to mitigate the final situation and are depleted financially and psychologically. They see no solution. Clinicians misdiagnose alienated parents as having a personality disorder because of the suicidal ideation, anger, grief, and victimization. However, these circumstances are real. Alienated parents are experiencing the loss of their children, and what could cause more of an emotional reaction in a parent?

Acceptance of the finality of losing one's children does not come easily. At times, parents are never able to accept the reality of the situation. Some parents are able to create a new life, find a new partner and perhaps have more children. Other parents take to understanding the dynamics of parent alienation and help other targeted parents. Moving on and creating a new life is the only viable option. When there is support from others and the alienated parent's realization that they were the best parent they could be and most likely did nothing egregious to deserve the ramifications of having left an unhappy marriage, they are able to "move on." But there are many steps to take before this happens.

SEEKING HELP

Understanding what's happening, and seeking help at the first stage is critical. At this time, the parent is traumatized, and it is important they have someone, preferably a trained therapist, to listen patiently to them. The clinical or other helping professional's purpose should be to listen and understand the experience of the alienated parent. An alienated parent, who is suffering from PTSD, repeats details of the trauma until they finally feel more in control and are able to organize the details of their experience. Keeping the alienated parent organized should be a high priority of the clinician or other helping professional. It is important that they listen, reassure, and educate, allowing them to spew all the details, sometimes over and over again. The key at this stage is to make sure the chosen therapist or clinician has been professionally trained to recognize that parental alienation is occurring. It is through this process that the targeted parent will be able to calm themselves, feel supported and begin to organize their minds, so they may then organize their legal case.

Targeted parents need to be encouraged to **not** write letters or have communication with anyone during the early stages, because their state of hysteria will reflect badly on them. Anything they do or say can and will be used against them by the alienator. If they appear to be unstable, even for a brief time, it will be described in detail, used to diagnose them, and documented over and over again in the most negative light, taking on a life of its own. Remember, alienators are master manipulators who frequently use gaslighting techniques to bait the targeted parent. Don't take the bait, especially in court.

ADVICE FOR THE THERAPIST

As a therapist, this is not the time to judge and criticize or have your own epiphanies regarding the alienation. An alienated parent needs unconditional acceptance and support.

They need the opportunity and the help to organize their thoughts and feelings about what happened, so they are able to present as cool, calm, convincing, and charming, and avoid displaying any of the four A's (anxious, agitated, angry, or afraid).

Diagnosing an alienated parent with a personality disorder is a grievous mistake, with severe consequences, according to a recent article, "Targeted Parents Surviving Parental Alienation: Consequences of the Alienation and Coping Strategies," published in the *Journal of Child and Family Studies*.[10]

Practitioners should assess the targeted parent's suicidal risk early in the treatment. They should also have an understanding that targeted parents experience trauma as a genuine reaction to their predicament, and when they lose contact with their children, they suffer ambiguous loss (unresolved grief) which can then lead to disenfranchised grief (grief not acknowledged by society).

Psychologist and author Craig Childress calls it, the "psychological killing of a parent" and he describes how it feels below:

> *"It's like (the alienator) murdered my children . . . but the only thing is I can't grieve. I can't go to a grave. I can't say anything that I want to say."*

---

[10] Saulyn Lee-Maturana, Mandy L. Matthewson, and Corinna Dwan, "Targeted Parents Surviving Parental Alienation: Consequences of the Alienation and Coping Strategies," *Journal of Child and Family Studies*, (May 2020).

Parental alienation is the most painful experience a parent can face, often without the support and understanding of family and friends. Their children are alive, yet lost to them. They feel shocked, desperate, confused and alone. They are frustrated, angry and fearful, due to the lack of understanding from those closest to them and from those who are meant to support and assist them. There is no joy left in their lives.

Chapter 6

Choosing Your
Support Network

"While heeding the profit of my counsel, avail yourself also of any helpful circumstances over and beyond the ordinary rules."

– Sun Tzu

THE PSYCHOTHERAPIST

I strongly recommend attending therapy before you hire a lawyer if you possibly can. However, research shows that engaging a therapist who is not familiar with the dynamics of parental alienation, is generally worse than not seeking the help of a therapist at all—so it is really important to be selective and choose someone with the right skill set.

I'm often asked how to find a therapist who is knowledgeable and competent with regards to PA. Here are three ways to find potential candidates:

- Start with a google search of "parental alienation therapists." If asked, many therapists will say they are familiar with parent alienation, when they actually are not. Finding one who specifically lists it as an area of expertise is a good safeguard against this.

- For recommendations on a suitably qualified therapist, you could contact a specialist PA group or organization, such as Parent Alienation Study Group, Parent Alienation Support and Intervention, or Family Access: Fighting for Children's Rights. You could also try searching for a Facebook group close to you who may be able to recommend someone in your area.

- Contact PA "experts" directly and ask them for a recommendation. In these days of Zoom and video consulting, getting therapy from a leader in the field is more accessible and acceptable than ever, and your physical location should not be a barrier.

Once you've found some potential candidates, contact them and ask them directly what they know about parent alienation. As a guide, they should be able to explain what

Choosing Your Support Network

it is and discuss the well-known factors at play, such as the counterintuitive nature, symptoms noted in children, etc. If they seem vague or can't tell you anything you didn't pick up yourself doing a quick online search, it's unlikely they have a deep understanding. You should also become familiar with the main theorists and experts, and ask the therapist which books they have read on the subject. There is a Further Reading list at the back of this book which is a good place to start. Any therapist on your shortlist should at least be familiar with Dr. Amy Baker, one of the foremost researchers of PA. Others who are prominent in the field include Dr. Richard Gardner, Dr. Richard Warshak, Dr. William Bernet, Dr. Michael Evans, Dr. J. Michael Bone, Dr. Steve Miller, Dr. Demosthenes Lorandos, Linda Gottlieb, LMFT, LCSW as well as Karen and Nick Woodall.

Here are some more questions to ask any potential therapists, to determine if they have a sound knowledge and understanding of PA:

- *What percentage of your time is spent working with alienated parents and children?*
- *Can you describe how an alienating parent behaves?*
- *What does the term counterintuitive mean?*
- *Have you been to any conferences on the subject? If so, which ones?* Parent Alienation Study Group (PASG) and Family Access, are two of the primary conference organizers.
- *Are you familiar with the eight symptoms of parental alienation in children?* These were written by Richard Gardner, M.D. thirty-five years ago and are well

63

known by therapists and other experts in parental alienation.

- *Are you familiar with the Parent Alienation Study Group (PASG)?* Headed by child psychiatrist, William Bernet, M.D., Professor Emeritus at Vanderbilt University, this is a key organization that anyone with a good working knowledge of PA should be aware of.

Another support option available is a parent alienation coach. However, they are pricey and are not required to undertake extensive training. A licensed, experienced therapist who is trained in parent alienation will be far more valuable. If you are considering a coach, ask them upfront, "On what basis do you consider yourself an expert in parental alienation?" as well as all the above mentioned questions, to be sure their help will be of value.

THE LAWYER

The important thing to remember when choosing your lawyer, is that you are the consumer. Ask them as many questions as you need to, until you feel confident that they are knowledgeable and experienced with parent alienation and the law.

In every instance, the first thing you should do is confirm that they are a family law attorney. Check with the State Bar Association to establish they do indeed belong to the Family Law Attorneys Association. I have seen parents who paid out large amounts of money, only to discover the attorney they are paying is not a family law attorney and is just going to court to collect their fees. Meanwhile, much valuable time is lost as the alienation continues to progress.

When choosing a lawyer, it's always helpful to get referrals from a trusted source—but you should also do your homework. Since PA cases are public domain once in court, if you are the researching type, you can search online to find out what the lawyer has said in previous cases.

Just like your therapist, you need to be sure your chosen lawyer has the right skill set. Start by asking some basic questions such as:

- Are you familiar with parental alienation?
- How did you receive your training in PA?
- What percentage of your practice deals with parental alienation cases?
- What are the eight symptoms of alienation identified by Richard Gardner, M.D.?
- What is your existing knowledge of previous cases of parental alienation? For example, do you know about the Neurater case? And are you aware that the American Bar Association published a book on parent alienation, *Children Held Hostage: Identifying Brainwashed Children*?

You should also discuss with them how they would feel if you were to hire a parental alienation expert to provide advice on how to properly represent an alienated parent.

Would they be willing to work with the expert or would they see it as a problem?

CHILDREN'S COURT

You are likely to be assigned to Children's (or Juvenile) Court if there have been abuse charges filed against you and the children have been removed to a foster home. A caseworker with Children's Protective Services is usually assigned. You can also request a lawyer who is pro bono (free), however, these lawyers are overworked and are not necessarily knowledgeable about parent alienation.

The caseworkers appointed to cases can be a nightmare. Some seem to care about the children entrusted to them and try to do the best for them. However, the majority of caseworkers are not trained to understand psychological reports and/or situations. They have far more control over families than should ever have been afforded them.

To highlight just one experience I had with a caseworker (and I have had many), a ten-year-old girl was removed from her mother's care after the stepfather molested her. He was immediately arrested and incarcerated, and the mother cut off all ties with him. The girl was placed with a foster parent who alienated the child against her mother. Being an expert in both sexual abuse and alienation, I recommended the girl be returned to her mother, with appropriate therapy. The caseworker thwarted every attempt at reconciliation and lied about the mother. She appeared to me to have an inappropriate relationship with the foster mother. The child is now sixteen and has never been returned to her mother. The judge most often sides with the caseworker despite all the evidence to indicate their decision is harmful to the child.

Most alienated parents are so intimidated by the involvement of the caseworkers, they capitulate to whatever the worker demands. However, you **do not** have to accommodate them. You can refer them to your lawyer. In my experience, caseworkers have little education and even less knowledge about parent alienation. They can be resistant to any attempts to teach them and they try to exert their self-appointed authority in cases.

Caseworkers do not have a right to choose or talk to your therapist, expert witness or your reconciliation therapist. You do not have to give them that information. They, and other court appointed professionals, are frequently seduced by, and enmeshed with, the alienator, and will defer to them.

A mother I worked with lost custody of her son to his father because she "was too emotional." The father had been diagnosed as a sociopath in a psychological test, and had spent four years in jail. This mom was in the constant position of defending against false accusations that both the boy's therapist and caseworker believed despite being unsubstantiated. She was constantly treated as if she was the guilty party. The caseworker who placed the child with a stepmother who had been convicted of child abuse and the father, a felon with a long history of deception, said they are "nice people." In my experience, they are simply unqualified to make such important decisions as to where a child should live.

As mentioned above, many caseworkers know very little (if anything) about parent alienation, yet they will assume unfounded authority in cases. They do not have this right, so refer them to your lawyer.

In his book, *Worst Interests of the Child*, award-winning investigative journalist Keith Harmon Snow exposes corruption within US family courts, stating: "No child in America is safe. On the Department of Family and Child Services' watch, each year, hundreds of thousands of children suffer from abuse (including rape and prolonged torture) at the hands of the parent with whom they are placed, or a foster parent. That would not happen without the corrupt practices taking place in CPS and Family Court."[11]

FAMILY COURT

If you are already involved in (or have previously experienced) a high conflict divorce you will be familiar with the Family Court. At the time of writing this book, most judges are not overly knowledgeable about parental alienation. Frustratingly, they frequently rule for the alienator who is *cool, calm, convincing, and charming.*

---

[11] Keith Harmon Snow, *Worst Interests of the Child*, (San Diego: Burning Sage Publications, 2015).

Unfortunately, at times, judges will state they do not want to hear about parental alienation. Your attorney is your advocate. Talk about this ahead of time and ask them how they would deal with this. The best option in this scenario is to **describe** the incidents that have already occurred that prove alienation. Describe your children's symptoms and be prepared to back up the information. Your attorney can ask specific questions of your expert witness that scientifically establishes parental alienation. The expert should also be able to cite studies on PA, and how it can be proven.

When **you** are in control and can dispute the false accusations without losing **your** composure, the alienator will most often be the one to lose **theirs**. You have to expose them. This is how you create a level playing field.

Some parents decide to represent themselves. It is not a good idea to go into court without an attorney. Most alienators have the resources to hire lawyers. Hiring an attorney who knows about parent alienation will reduce the amount of court time, and even if they are outrageously expensive, it might help prevent the loss of your children and save money and heartache in the long run. If you have to hire a less expensive lawyer, make sure the lawyer is amenable to consulting with an expert on PA (of your choosing) who could provide your case with the stamp of authenticity you will need in court.

In children's or dependency court, the children are represented, and not the parent, so filing a contempt of custody/court orders does not apply. Having the case closed and transferring to Family Court would be more advantageous for an alienated parent.

GOING "PRO SE" OR "ACTING ON ONE'S OWN BEHALF"

In her book *Dismantling the Family Court Corruption: Why Taking the Kids was Not Enough*, author Maryann Petri describes her experience:

> "To be honest, it was unnerving and stressful gathering the paperwork needed to put motions together. But, along the way, I had gotten a lot of helpful information from other attorneys on YouTube, such as, making four copies of all paperwork and keeping two copies in my file . . . I confidently walked into every courtroom conservatively dressed, with my head held high. It was important to show no fear, almost to the point of annoying the judge. Speaking the truth was challenging to the judge's authority, and I was threatened with jail."[12]

As Dr. Mark Roseman points out, "Those litigants who elect to represent themselves 'Pro Se' are frequently viewed by opposing counsel and, indeed the presiding judge, as impediments to the court process."

---

[12] Maryann Petri, *Dismantling the Family Court Corruption: Why Taking the Kids was Not Enough*, (Triumph Press, 2020).

The key to success is to continue despite all the discouragement and trauma. Judge Donald B. King once stated, "The role of the Family Court too often is to shoot the survivors." Maryann Petri defines legal abuse as, "an unfair legal action that has been initiated with malicious and selfish intentions." Legal abuse can originate from nearly any part of the legal system, the Department of Children's and Family Services (DCFS), frivolous and false accusations by the opposing parent, by family of the alienator, law enforcement, incompetent, careless or corrupt attorneys, GALs and even the judges themselves.

THE DOMESTIC RELATIONS DEPARTMENT or CHILD SUPPORT SERVICES

This is the department best known for their work enforcing child support payments. It is important to be well-prepared here and have a good working knowledge of what is fair and allowed. In past cases there has been examples of a judge deliberately setting inflated child support payments, for example, using the potential earnings rather than what is actually being earned. When the parent is unable to pay, they are labelled as a "deadbeat", their driver's license is confiscated, and they may go to jail.

GUARDIANS AD LITEM (GALs)

On the subject of guardians ad litem, attorney Ashish S. Joshi writes: "Family courts often appoint a guardian ad litem to represent the children's best interests in cases where parental alienation is alleged. While judges appoint lawyers as GALs, they make little effort to ensure that these professionals have had proper training to handle such cases. Despite the fact that PA is known to be a nuanced subject and also deeply counterintuitive, GALs more often than not rely on their professional intuition in resolving these complex cases. And intuition—*I've been doing this for a long time and I know exactly what's required here*— to solve complex counterintuitive problems is rarely, if ever, adequate. In cases involving PA, it can be downright disastrous."[13]

GALs, without any substantial knowledge of parent alienation are appointed, and are known to make recommendations to take away custody from the alienated parent, based purely on what the child has said (no matter how false and/or abusive it is) and allow the child to choose where they live. Of course, listening to the child is always recommended, but in PA situations, without proper training, it is incumbent upon GALs to consult with experts in the field to ensure they have a clear understanding of the what is really taking place.

In one situation I know of, a GAL recommended the children not see their mother despite the fact the mother had not been abusive in any way, and her ex lied to the judge repeatedly in court, no questions asked. In other situations, I've experienced GALs voluntarily attending PA conferences and training. Since it's entirely up to the GALs

---

[13] Desmosthenes Lorandos and William Bernet, *Parent Alienation – Science and the Law*, (Springfield: Charles C Thomas Publisher, 2020).

own discretion, you just never know how educated a GAL will be in PA. Passing a law to make parental alienation deemed as child abuse and making training for all GALs mandatory, is what needs to happen and is what I am currently working towards with various other PA experts.

MINOR'S COUNSEL

This is an attorney appointed by the court to represent the child (or children) only, and not the parents. Oftentimes a minor's counsel can be familiar with parental alienation and will work together with the parent's attorneys. They have the authority to, for example, recommend reunification therapy and the judge will concur. I have experienced minor's counsel to be willing to make recommendations based on parental alienation and their concern for the child. This is encouraging. I have also experienced minor's counsel to be oblivious to PA and do nothing to help the situation.

CUSTODY EVALUATORS

Custody evaluators are given the task of determining what is in the best interest of the child psychologically. If the courts appoint one to your case, you can interview the custody evaluator (who is usually a psychologist) about how familiar they are with parental alienation. Most will claim they are knowledgeable, but in reality, do not know enough to determine if alienation is taking place. Use the guidelines given above for questioning lawyers and therapists to question custody evaluators.

The first parental alienation case I worked with, where I could tell things were off, was when a mom, a teacher with six children ranging from five to twenty years of age came in, distraught about possibly losing her children. Upon interviewing the children, they tearfully claimed that they loved their mom, and hoped she would forgive them for what they were about to do. They would not say what that was. They could not think of anything their mom had done to cause them to be angry with her. It was a puzzle. When I contacted the custody evaluator, the problem became clear. The children described their mom as "strict", making them do their homework before they could play at the park, "making" them go to private schools, etc., etc. The eldest daughter complained her mother had pulled her out of the car once, a long time ago, when she refused to get out. Their father on the other hand, was "laid back", would let them go to school in their own neighborhood, play in the park anytime, was always around. Their neighborhood was a gang infested area, from which the mom wanted to protect her children. She did not want them dressed in gang attire. The father worked at home, fixing cars and was ostensibly agoraphobic, so could not go to court, therapy, schools, or anywhere else a parent would normally have to go to support his children. He prided himself on not paying taxes. He left at least ten threatening messages for me while I was seeing the children and their mother.

You may have guessed by now that the evaluator recommended the father get full custody of the children.

Custody evaluators can be biased and ignorant regarding parental alienation. However, the courts will usually agree to have at least three names from both parents and the court will choose one, so do your research and put forward the names of the best evaluators you can find. Go online and check their reviews. If they are less than professional, the reviews on Yelp, licensing boards, and other online review sites will give you plenty of information. It's well worth the effort, as a custody evaluator who knows about parental alienation is worth their weight in gold.

EXPERT TESTIMONY

Experts can be the element of change that is needed in PA cases. They gather all the court documents available, including all relevant information such as police reports, school reports, therapist's reports, medical letters etc., and write a report that proves alienation and testifies to their findings.

In their book *Parental Alienation – Science and Law*, authors William Bernet and Demosthenes Lorandos state that an expert must be able to explain:

- The science, methodology, and criteria for the diagnosis of parental alienation
- The presence and evidence of alienation
- The best method of treatment to stop the alienation[14]

---

[14] Desmosthenes Lorandos and William Bernet, *Parent Alienation – Science and the Law*, (Springfield: Charles C Thomas Publisher, 2020).

When considering the use of an expert witness in court, ask yourself these questions:

- Will expert testimony help the court understand PA?
- Is the expert knowledgeable and qualified in the field of PA?
- Could the information given by the expert be misused and harm you?
- Does the expert have sufficient knowledge of the family to provide valid testimony?
- Is the expert knowledgeable of the theory, technique, or methodology and can they apply this knowledge to PA?

The way different experts prepare will vary, according to what they have found most successful in the past when giving their testimony. The process I have found that works consistently well is to thoroughly read all the court documents, police reports, treating therapists' reports, custody evaluations, psychological tests, visitation monitor reports and any other pertinent information. I then prepare a comprehensive report, using all objective information, as well as proof of false reports, and dispel accusations that have become "facts" throughout court hearings.

I prepare a contract for the judge to use with the alienator to prevent them from interfering in the reconciliation between the alienated parent and child, as well as a table of consequences for the alienator if they do not obey court orders or try to sabotage the reconciliation. For this I use

"Three Strikes You're Out", developed by Joan Kloth-Zanard, whereby on the third violation, custody is transferred to the alienated parent.

An important aspect of being an expert witness is to address the tendency of the court to claim a child should be able to choose where they live, especially if they are fourteen or older. This is ludicrous from a psychological point of view. Alienated children are not "advanced" or "mature enough to decide." In fact, it's quite the opposite. They are often arrested, developmentally speaking, at the stage when the alienation started.

A judge can understand a child's decision to not see a parent is impaired, but acquiesces "because one cannot force a child to live with a parent they state they do not want to."

OR

A judge can say, "It is not your parent's decision where you live, but the court's, and both you and your parents have to abide by the order."

An expert can request this in the report, and order the DCFS worker and both parents and all interested parties to support this, and the child will comply.

The whole objective of going to the trouble and turmoil of going to court is to reconcile the child with the alienated parent and to determine a just custody situation which is in the best interests of the child.

Once it has been established that a child is alienated, the next step is to arrange the reconciliation therapy. No child is better off with one parent, **unless,** as previously explained, there is **proven** abuse, a **pattern** of abuse by a parent, there is no need to remove a child from a parent's custody. Although children do not reach a legal age until they turn eighteen, they still do not have certain privileges that involve best judgment. There also has to be emotional evidence of abuse. If alienated children do not demonstrate that they are being abused, and their behavior does not show the evidence of abuse there may be false accusations. For example, after claiming sexual abuse, they do not exhibit the usual behavior a sexually abused child might.

The following is a well-known case where horrendous child abuse was committed.

A young boy in California, Gabriel Fernandez, was appallingly abused by his mother and stepfather. DCFS and the police visited the home several times due to reports from family and the school. The mother convinced them Gabriel was "fine" and lied a lot. The social workers and police reprimanded Gabriel, intimidating him by doing it in a police car. Social workers did not go in, did not visit the school and most often only talked to the mother.

Gabriel's schoolteacher described him as a bright, friendly, empathic child who came to school with cuts, bruises and other wounds. He was depressed and hopeless and asked for help. But afterwards said he felt afraid because he was inevitably retaliated against by his parents for reporting the abuse.

His mom and stepfather beat Gabriel relentlessly, kept him in a closet, bound and gagged, didn't feed him and dressed him in girls' clothes because the stepfather decided he was gay—at eight years old. They killed this lovely child. The social workers have since had to defend charges made against them for their neglect. The police "have handled the situation internally." There is now a documentary on Netflix about Gabriel.

In alienation situations, the child is not able to manufacture symptoms of being abused because they do not know what the symptoms are. They are absent. One boy's alienating father called DCFS to report he was crying outside of the house with scratches and cuts caused by his mom. When the worker arrived, mom was inside cleaning and the boy eventually returned from school, happy, and communicative, showing no evidence of abuse.

DCFS and police can, on occasions, be slack and downright wrong. They are not qualified to determine the presence of alienation, so retaining an expert can be what turns a case around. Get a recommendation for a qualified expert. They should have a degree and experience in being an expert witness. Having a good memory is also a plus, as I was recently able to contradict a judge and GAL when they gave misinformation, based on what I had read in the documents!

REUNIFICATION THERAPISTS

Many therapists claim to be a reunification therapist, but often they do not even know what alienation is! Again, don't be afraid to ask questions to determine the true extent of their knowledge of PA. Use the questions listed earlier in the chapter to interview any potential therapist. Ask the therapist and if they do not know about alienation, do not pursue therapy with them. Being in therapy with a therapist who does not understand the counterintuitive nature of alienation could be worse for an alienated parent and child than having no therapy at all. Co-parenting therapy does not work when there is alienation occurring and one hour a week with an untrained therapist will do more harm than good. The child needs to be out of the alienator's environment and therapy should be at a minimum two hours long weekly. Linda Gottlieb insists the reunification therapy will not work if the child is not transferred into the alienated parent's custody for at least ninety days. I agree that is the optimal situation, but will work with what I can get and have still had success, using her method of empowering the alienated parent.

Most programs claim a high success rate. Considering the differences, I was curious about these claims. Now I realize it is quite easy to get a child to reconcile with a once-loved parent when the alienator is removed from the situation. Children want the relationship with their alienated parent, in spite of what they say.

Recently, a child supposedly requested to be interviewed by the court to be allowed to tell them he hated his mother and did not want to see her. Both the therapist and expert strongly recommended this not be allowed because of the damage to the child. Custody for the mother was increased, and the son happily called his mother all weekend long to discuss various subjects with her.

In summary, it is especially important to go to a qualified, ethical, and well-trained reconciliation therapist. There are specialized programs throughout the country, and traveling to a different location is a good idea so as to make it more difficult for the alienator to interfere.

Therapists who operate within the traditional "Family Systems" version of psychotherapy think that reunification therapy should be coordinated with social workers and other therapists involved. In my opinion, reunification therapy should be conducted without the involvement of other professionals, and certainly without the alienator. There has already been too much involvement with the courts and various other agencies. Reunification therapy should be preserved for the alienated parent and child.

Here is an excerpt from a social worker's recommendation to the court, who claims to be an expert in reunification therapy:

> "At this time, this clinician is not recommending reunification services for [dad and son]. [Son] is not willing to participate. (My note: No alienated children are willing to participate in therapy that is so threatening to the alienator, that is why the

judge has to order the therapy). It is a general rule in reunification therapy that children do not respond to being forced to adhere to the demands of a parent with whom they have a difficult history. This is particularly true of adolescents."(My note: Most often, the previously close relationship, without the interference from the alienator, can be quickly reestablished).

Parent alienation expert and reunification specialist, Linda Gottlieb, LMFT, LCSW, has a four-day intervention program called Turning Points, and an almost perfect success rate. Her objective is to train as many qualified therapists as possible to use this method. I use her method and find it to be very successful in reuniting alienated parents and children. I do follow the family for a year to ensure success and provide more intervention if necessary. To date, all the reunifications have succeeded for a full year following the intervention, and this includes families with children of all ages, as well as adult children.

ADA ADVOCATES

It is possible to be declared disabled when diagnosed with PTSD as a result of being traumatized through alienation. In such cases, an Americans with Disabilities Advocate is entitled to sit in a court hearing and mediation and be a witness to the hearing. Their purpose is to make sure the clients get the services to which they are entitled during the hearing. In a recent court hearing the ADA advocate reported the judge for being abusive, forcing the judge to recuse himself. The alienated parent had not been able to do this in the many years she had fought "pro se" for her children.

The primary thrust here is to choose qualified professionals at all stages and to be a consumer about your choice. It will pay off in the long run.

Chapter 7

What To Expect In Court

"Move not until you see an advantage; use not your troops unless there is something to be gained; fight not unless the position is critical."

– Sun Tzu

*I*f you're an alienated parent, it is highly likely you will need to take your case to the courts at some stage to reach a custody resolution. This would most likely be to change your custody or visitation arrangements, to file a motion for contempt, or to request a restraining order. In this chapter we will look closely at some of the terminology, procedures and requirements that are part of the court process, to give you an idea of what to expect. It is intended as a guide for those who wish to represent themselves (pro se), but even if you have a lawyer representing you, it is important to have an understanding of what is happening at all stages of your case. That way, you can prepare yourself in the best possible way.

Despite the fact that there is currently no law against parental alienation in the USA and numerous other countries, parental alienation is recognized in courts and can be proven.

Proving parental alienation can be accomplished by an expert and by a lawyer that is educated on the subject.

Disclaimer: I am not a lawyer, so I am not in a position to provide legal advice. The contents of this chapter are general information only, observed over many years of working as an expert witness in cases involving parental alienation. The legal information within is intended as a guide only, please seek expert advice regarding your own situation.

HIRING A LAWYER VS. PRO SE (REPRESENTING YOURSELF)

To be pro se means that you are representing yourself in a legal proceeding. Pro se can also be referred to as being in propria persona (pro per) in parts of the country.

As previously stated, I don't think representing yourself is the ideal situation. Typically, you will be held to the same standards as an attorney. If you do represent yourself, it is imperative to file the correct forms in a timely fashion, serve them appropriately, and know the basics of the legal process. If you can't afford an attorney, I highly suggest that every step of the way you confer with a paralegal, or at minimum, scour your local courthouse's website for the appropriate forms and procedures, and procure any legal advice you can. If you're specifically dealing with an alienation case and are unable to retain an expert witness, consulting with one would be the next best option.

Hiring a lawyer is strongly recommended over going per se, however, as mentioned in the previous chapter, be sure they have an in-depth knowledge of parental alienation. There are attorneys out there who are experts in PA, so ideally work with them. If it is not possible to hire an expert PA lawyer for your case, try and find one who may be willing consult with you and your lawyer to broaden your knowledge. They may be willing to provide guidance on what to expect and how to best approach things, based on their experience.

PETITIONER AND RESPONDENT

Whether you have an attorney or not, the person who files the first motion is known as the Petitioner, while the one responding is referred to as the Respondent. That means if you initially filed for divorce and/or custody, you will always be the Petitioner. Even if there are subsequent filings by the Respondent, you will still be considered the Petitioner.

COMPLETING AND FILING PAPERWORK

No matter your reason for attending court, the first step is always to correctly complete and lodge the required paperwork. When you engage a lawyer they will make sure all the paperwork is completed and filed correctly on your behalf, but if you are pro se, you are responsible for this yourself. It is vital that it is done correctly, so do your research and pay careful attention to what is required.

You can visit the Court Service Center to find out about the forms you will need, however, keep in mind the resources and knowledge of the service center staff may only extend to basic filings. Knowing the foundations of family law in your state yourself, is essential if you are pro se. Search your local courthouse website for details on the steps to follow when you file, but a few fundamentals to keep in mind are:

- Know your case number, which can be found on the court website under "Family Law" and "case access"
- If printing your documents, always use "pleading paper" which is a numbered paged template. The template is easily found on a google search. The courts will only accept filings that are on this paper
- A standard twelve point font is required and your spacing must be 1.5
- If you have any exhibits, they must be numbered and shown on a separate piece of paper before the exhibit

Once you have located the right forms for your case, fill them in carefully, following the instructions on the form **exactly**. Double check the information is correct, then sign them and make three additional copies. You are now ready to lodge the forms, which can be done in person or by mail.

If you file in person, bring all four copies with you to the courthouse that made your current custody or visitation orders and give your completed forms to the clerk. The clerk will hand write a hearing date and time on the Motion and stamp it with the date you filed it. The stamped copies are now considered "conformed" copies. The copy with your original signature goes to the judge, one copy is for you, one copy is for your ex and, and the other is considered a "courtesy" copy for the courtroom.

If you file by mail, be sure to include a self-addressed stamped envelope so your conformed copies can be sent back to you. With regards to your hearing date, don't be surprised if it is three months away—that is pretty standard. Always keep a record of the papers you have filed with the court. A good way to do this is to scan the conformed copies and save them on your computer.

You are also required to give (or serve) a copy of the Motion to your ex. Ask the court if they have any specific rules about who may serve the form, but generally you can use a marshal, a sheriff, a registered process server, or a friend who is not a party to the action, is over the age of eighteen, and is not a protected person listed in any of the orders.

The court can provide a list of marshals and sheriffs, or you can often find this listed on their website too. A registered process server may be used for a nominal fee. A quick search on Google will provide a list of some in your area. Whoever you choose to serve the forms, they must identify the party being served and physically hand the papers to him/her and inform them that they are court papers. If the party being served does not want to take the paper, they can be left on the ground in front of them. The person being served does not have to sign anything. One client I had made sure her server video recorded the service and it was a good thing because in court, her ex's attorney claimed they were never served. My client was able to provide proof that her ex's attorney attempted to deceive the judge.

Your proof of service needs to be signed and dated by the person who served the other parent. You will need to make two copies, one for you and one for filing with the court. Be sure to scan this to your computer as well.

TIPS FOR ATTENDING COURT

Attending court can make you feel nervous or anxious, and while this is normal, try and stay calm and in control at all times. Aim to get to court at least thirty minutes early, as you'll need time to find parking, get through security, find your courtroom and take a breath so you walk in as calm, cool, and confident as your ex.

When you arrive, there should be a printed page of the day's hearings taped next to the door of your courtroom. Find your case number. This is not your actual case number, it's the numeric order of the court hearings that day. Typically, the ex parte hearings—emergency hearings—are heard first. Once you see your number, enter the court room and tell the clerk what your number is, identify yourself as either the Petitioner or Respondent and wait to be heard. I suggest you sit in the courtroom to wait so you can listen to the cases before yours. You may glean insight to your judge's likes or dislikes.

When your case is called, you will be invited to take your seat before the judge. Here are some tips to keep in mind which may help you during the proceeding:

- When responding to questions, speak slowly, give complete answers, and tell the truth
- If anything is unclear, don't be afraid to ask for clarification
- Be polite, don't argue and try not to get upset. Remember the four A's and avoid them
- Don't interrupt others and only speak to the judge when it is your turn
- Refer to the judge as "Your Honor," and the attorney as "Counsel"
- Refer to the other parent as "Petitioner" or "Respondent" whichever he/she is
- Make detailed notes as needed, especially when the judge is giving an order

GOING OFF THE RECORD

It's also important to be aware that at times during the hearing you may go off the record, which means the court reporter is no longer transcribing the conversation. If that happens, the judge will tell you. If something important is decided during that time, be sure to repeat it **on the record**.

One of my clients had an experience where they went off the record to discuss holiday schedules and vacation dates. During that time, my client asked the judge if she could take their child on a trip that weekend, her ex's weekend. The judge then asked her ex if that would be okay. Her ex responded with, "Of course, Your Honor. I'm totally okay with that." Because it was done off the record, it did not make it into the minute order or the Order After Hearing. My client then took their child on that trip. Her ex and his attorney then filed contempt charges against her for taking their child out of state without his permission during "his days." She had to get an attorney and fight the charges. They were eventually dismissed, but it cost her $17,000 in attorney's fees to fight it.

DOES YOUR CHILD NEED A LAWYER?

A lawyer for your child is also known as a Minor's Counsel. If you think you may want one for your child, you can make a request to the judge. This may be appropriate if you and the other parent disagree about custody or visitation, you are worried about your child's safety (if there is substance abuse, child abuse, or domestic violence), or there is a question about paternity.

The court can appoint a lawyer for your child, and depending on their age, they will either act as an Attorney for the Minor Child (AMC) or a Guardian Ad Litem (GAL). It is their job to tell the court their recommendations on what they believe is best for your child (and if they are older, what your child wants). They will also recommend how to best handle conflicts, and how you as parents can best meet the child's needs. They will base their recommendations on their observations of the child during meetings, as well as from their meetings with you, the other parent and other adults involved in caring for the child such as teachers or doctors. They will also view medical records and if appropriate arrange for physical and mental health assessments.

MEDIATION

If you have a court-ordered visitation arrangement in place that is not working, the first step is to get in touch with the mediation office in the courthouse where your case was first heard. They can arrange to meet with you and the other parent and try and sort out the problem in mediation.

Your mediator will make recommendations, but you do not have to agree if you are not content with the terms. If the problem can't be solved in mediation, the next step is to return to court to request a change to your custody or visitation order.

WHEN WILL THE JUDGE MAKE A DECISION?

The judge often decides cases at the end of the hearing and announces the order(s) in the courtroom while you are still there. If this happens, before you go off the record, repeat the orders back to the judge to be clear. As mentioned earlier, alienators are notorious for finding loopholes and if you're in pro se, you want to be sure that your ex or his/her counsel doesn't twist things in their favor in the Order After Hearing (OAH). This has happened to one of my clients and she had to then pay for the transcript, write an objection to their OAH, file her own OAH, and have the judge sign her's.

Occasionally, the judge will want some extra time to decide, in which case they will say, "I'll take the papers." Once the judge has reviewed the files and made a decision, the clerk will mail you a copy of the judge's orders. If you don't hear from the court after a few days, call the clerk and ask about your case. It's also a good idea to ask the court reporter for their business card before you leave the courtroom, in case you need to purchase the transcript.

Going to court can be extremely stressful if you're pro se and it can be very time consuming to prepare court documents. My advice for you is to do everything you can to keep all court documents and proceedings out of sight and earshot of your child. Don't leave papers on the table where they can be seen or read. Don't talk about court on the phone when you child is present. Their ears suddenly become bionic and they hear everything. Resist the urge to bad mouth the other parent to your child or in earshot. Don't tell them information about the court. It is in their best interests to not be involved in what is often a really challenging and confronting process. If you need to talk to someone about what is happening, confide in someone you trust, or seek out professional support services in your state.

Chapter 8

Proving Parental Alienation

"Be extremely subtle, even to the point of formlessness. Be extremely mysterious, even to the point of soundlessness. Thereby you can be the director of the opponent's fate."

– Sun Tzu

*I*n court, the judge will read a short report that is evidence-based and not hearsay. Evidence can consist of therapist's reports, monitors of visitation reports, police reports, school reports, letters from friends or family or other interested and fairly objective parties that have seen your parenting and have something positive to say. Preparing a strong report with the help of an expert can be a key factor in how your case is viewed and judged in court.

It is especially important to pick out remarks that have been made identifying parental alienation. For example, in court documents a judge may admonish the alienator by saying, "If alienation is proven here, I am transferring custody" or "There is obviously severe alienation taking place." These statements are then buried in the court documents, so using them can be extremely useful.

More than once I have examined psychological tests and found the resulting scales do not match the diagnosis and analysis the psychologist offers. For example, results mentioning sociopathy is not mentioned, or conversely an alienated parent is diagnosed as narcissistic and sociopathic, but there is no evidence for the diagnosis in the psychological tests. Using an expert (usually one with a PhD degree since they are trained in psychological measurements) who can read psychological test results can be helpful in disputing a negative result.

More often than not I have found an alienated parent accused of abuse when there is NO abuse. Upon researching the source of the accusation, it turns out to be a onetime incident where there are no bruises, no marks in fact, that become a charge of abuse. (For example, grabbing a kicking child by the hair, and not on purpose). Suddenly, the alienated child is afraid of that parent, does not feel "safe" with the alienated parent, and collapses in hysteria at the sight of the rejected parent's car. Presenting how one incident became abuse is compelling evidence for a judge who will decide if there is alienation taking place.

The letter that follows, was shared by an alienated mother. It is from a grandmother (mother of the alienator) to her granddaughter who is an alienated child. It is an example of how a child is influenced to hate their parent for no good reason.

"Hi –

I'm sorry I did not get to talk to you when I called back. And I'm sorry for how the conversation went with your father. (Father is living with his parents).

All I was trying to say is that there may be a way for you to leave the city (if that is what you want) when you're sixteen. I am not saying it is absolute but I operate very differently from your father.

I may be off but I believe that both you and your father are giving your mother this great power. She is not Wonder Woman. She is a confused unstable person who only has her motherhood left and she's determined to use her control. So when you go there, you don't talk to her. You go to your friends', you stay late at school, sleepover with friends. That's what teenagers do anyway. You won't see her.

I get that your dad doesn't want you to have false hope. I get that. But I think you know that there are no guarantees and that all you can do is try to do what you think best. Bottom line you will focus on you and your studies and try to remove yourself from your mother. Please do not let your mother define the years. She is not worth it.

99

So have a fun July 4th. We are planning on doing nothing which is fine with me.

Be well, enjoy yourself. Do not give into sadness.

Love, Grandma."

This is one of 192 emails. This is what a campaign by the alienators looks like. Subtle but not so subtle. Keep these kinds of letters as evidence of the campaign against you and the evidence of the advice children get from alienators.

To prove alienation is taking place, it is important to document what is happening with the alienating behavior. Some ideas on how you can do this include:

Keep a record of dates and events: Use a diary or journal to record the dates, times and reasons when you were denied access to your child by the other parent. Be sure to include all the details around the situation and the excuses used. Record all the details, as you never know what information may prove to be important later. Having a consistent and specific record of what has taken place may prove to be very helpful in court, as it shows habitual alienating behavior over time.

Always put all correspondence about the child in writing: When parental alienation is taking place, it's essential that you use text messages and emails when asking to see your child. That way you have written evidence you can show the court that proves your desire and efforts to see your child and demonstrates that alienation is taking place. Avoid verbal requests over the phone or in person, instead, always put it in writing in a text message or email, as alienators will often deny any such conversations ever took place. When it is all in writing, you can show that your ex uses the same excuses for denying visits, despite your continued requests.

Attend counseling: Seeing a therapist not only helps you in coping with the alienation, it will also help to support to your case if you go to court. Showing that you are being proactive and taking steps to improve the situation will help to strengthen your case. You may even wish to invite your ex to attend. Even if they decline, it will signal to the courts that you are making every effort to work together and co-parent effectively.

Don't give up: When your ex continually denies you the chance to see your child, it is absolutely frustrating and upsetting. If you are being denied or ignored, despite your best efforts it can seem like you are wasting your time. But it's essential that you keep the bigger picture in mind—your child needs you. Don't give up! If you give up, you provide the alienator with exactly what they want, which is to paint you as a parent who doesn't care. Be persistent, keep trying and seek support if you need it. Your efforts are not in vain.

Working with an expert in parental alienation will help you prepare for court and decide which records are important and what you should present to the court. Other helpful reports to keep include:

- visitation monitors
- school reports
- psychological reports
- police reports
- letters from friends and family supporting you and making observations about what they have seen
- photographs, cards, letters and videos that show you had a loving relationship prior to separation and divorce
- notes about a lack of cards and invitations sent to you for special occasions (e.g. birthdays, mother's/fathers' day, graduations) since the alienation.

These documents can be helpful in reunification therapy as well. They can be used to show the alienated child the loving relationship that once existed between the parent and child.

Although the communication platforms, Talking Parents, and Our Family Wizard, have been set up by the court for communication **between parents** regarding the children, anyone can use them. They both cost a nominal fee but are recommended because they track when a message was opened. This information can be essential for court if the other parent claims they never received a message. These platforms are not intended to be shown to the children as proof of the misconduct of the other parent! They allow you to go "no contact" with the alienator as much as you can and have all communication go through the court platform's texts. This will provide invaluable documentation about the alienation that is occurring.

As a victim of PA, you will likely find yourself in a position at some point where you are asked to defend that it exists, to family, friends, therapists, courts, and worst of all, your children. YOU DO NOT HAVE TO PUT YOURSELF IN THIS POSITION. Provide some examples of experts, names of books, and articles etc., but do not get into a situation where the onus is on you to prove there is parental alienation occurring. It exists, and has been well-documented, end of story. The courts in this country acknowledge the existence of parental alienation. In addition, both the United Nations and the World Health Organization have recognized alienation and condemned the practice of allowing one parent to be ejected from a child's life.

Instead of defending your position, turn it around on the naysayer by asking them to prove it is **not** alienation, given the circumstances.

Here are a few well-known examples of judges speaking about parental alienation that can help give you confidence.

- Judge Lisa Gorcyca states: *"Any lawyer, judge, mental health professional, or caseworker who has ANY involvement with the family court, is aware that one of the most devastating issues we face is that of parental alienation"*.

- Texas Supreme Court Judge Debra Lerhmann, Chair of the American Bar Association's Family

Law section says: *"Anyone who's in this business knows there are situations where that (parental alienation) is happening . . . "*

- The popular Judge Judy, a veteran of Family Court with her own TV show *Judge Judy*, has much to say on the subject of parental alienation on YouTube, where she states: *"A child has two parents. It is inappropriate for one parent to deprive the child the input from a second parent because they don't get along anymore. The departure is not relevant. The child has a right (to have two parents)."*

The persistence of a few to dismiss or discredit parental alienation does not stack up against the scientific evidence that confirms it is emotional abuse. It is important to arm yourself with the knowledge and confidence to deal with these comments as they arise. Below are some common examples the naysayers use that you may encounter:

Parental alienation is not in the *DSM-5*: This claim is simply misleading. First, the *DSM-5* (*The Diagnostic and Statistical Manual of Mental Disorders*) is used primarily by institutions—not to diagnose *syndromes*, but to diagnose *individuals*. Diagnoses for each member of the family is covered in the DSM, and so is Shared Delusional Disorder, which describes the child's adoption of the alienator's delusion regarding the rejected parent. Child Psychological Abuse, which describes the effects on the child, is also appropriately used. The American Psychiatric Association recognizes that once a child is removed from the alienator, the delusion disappears. Predictably behind the times and allergic to taking any risks, the American Psychological Association has "formed a committee" to study PA and child abuse![15]

There is no scientific evidence: A 2019 research study from Colorado University's Dr. Jennifer Harmon and colleagues put the incidence of parental alienation at around 1.5 percent of the population—which equates to approximately 22 million. The complaint that parental alienation is not scientifically proven and there are no research studies to support it is just bogus. There is a plethora of studies that have been conducted by well-respected researchers and are there for the reading.[16]

Labeling parental alienation as junk science: You may hear some (including attorneys) calling PA "junk science" or claiming "you are peddling snake oil." This is ludicrous. Expert witnesses can now say with certainty the research proves otherwise and can provide proof to back up what they are saying. Inquire what evidence they have that PA is "junk science." There are some excellent videos available to view online of Dr. William Bernet discussing how to deal with misinformation.[17]

---

[15] 15. American Psychiatric Association, *Diagnostic and Statistical Manual of Mental Disorders 5th Edition* (Arlington: American Psychiatric Publishing, 2013).

[16] Jennifer J. Harman, Sadie Leder-Elder, and Zeynep Biringer, "Prevalence of adults who are targets of parental alienating behaviors and their impact," *Children and Youth Services Review* 106 (November 2019).

[17] William Bernet, "Parental Alienation in the DSM-5," filmed 2010, New York, video, 1:01, https://www.youtube.com/watch?v=nA2AJRzJDAY

It is gender specific: Historically, fathers were frequently rejected from their children's lives because the mothers were routinely given custody of their children. The problem of parental alienation is no longer gender specific as more and more fathers fight for 50/50 custody of their children.

Children never lie: This is just ridiculous. Anyone who has children knows this is a fallacy. My three-year-old nephew, his cheeks stuffed like a chipmunk with candy, told his mother he had not been eating the candy. Children lie. My own teenage daughter told me she often lied to me to test my ability to catch her at it. It was a game to her, despite admonishments it was not appropriate or acceptable to lie. Alienated children are put in positions where they have to lie (e.g. mommy/daddy didn't tell me to do that). It is abusive to one's child to get them to cover up what is actually occurring in a home and creating false allegations against the rejected parent. Parents have gone to prison, innocent of criminal charges. The guilt children suffer later can be unbearable to them, often ending in suicide.

An extreme example comes from an inappropriately named group out of California, "Center for Judicial Excellence." They have been the recipients of a large government grant and often appear on television shows claiming parental alienation is junk science and that the founder of PA was a pedophile. This is patently untrue and they need to be confronted and demanded that they show proof of what they are claiming. They appeared at the California Psychological Association Board Meeting with a number of alienators, complaining about "PA psychologists" and demanding they lose their licenses (which has actually happened). The other request is that "parent alienation" be struck from the language! To their credit, the board cut the presentation short and moved on with their agenda. (You can view this on YouTube.)

COMMON MYTHS ABOUT ALIENATION

In his article in *Professional Psychology: Research and Practice*, Dr. Richard Warshak shared the following 10 myths regarding parental alienation:

1. **Children never unreasonably reject the parent with whom they spend the most time.** Evaluators and courts should be alert to the possibility that a child's rejection of a parent with whom they primarily live is unwarranted, and that the children should remain in that parent's custody while working to repair the relationship.

2. **Children never reasonably reject mothers.** Many unreasonably believe that "mothers must have done something terrible" to be rejected by their child, and the child must have good reasons for doing so. Mothers can be as easily and unreasonably alienated, just as much as fathers.

3. **Each parent contributes equally to a child's alienation.** "Favored" parents are more likely to have borderline and narcissistic psychopathology and are more likely to display controlling and coercive

behavior, poorly modulated rage, paranoid traits, and parenting styles that encourage enmeshed parent-child relationships.

4. **Alienation is a child's short-lived, transient response to the parents' separation.** The average length of time of an alienation is three to four years, and can be as much as twenty years, or even a lifetime. Therapists focus therapy on helping the child cope with unpleasant feelings they have toward the alienated parent, and "setting boundaries", primarily inappropriately. Trained PA therapists will focus on the alienated parent and child mending rifts so no more time is wasted.

5. **Rejecting a parent is a child's short-term healthy coping mechanism.** It is not in a child's best interest for professionals to exercise control over the situation or relieve themselves of loyalties by siding with one parent against the other, or by the child reducing discomfort by devaluing and avoiding contact with the rejected parent. Therapists who promote this alienation contribute to the child's alienation and subsequent impaired development. There is, rather, a need for early intervention and an enforcement of court orders to relieve the child's burden of feeling they have to choose between two beloved parents.

6. **Young children living with an alienating parent need no intervention.** The court should keep in mind the formative experience of young children

and ensure the child is able to develop a positive relationship with both parents. Children may need more time with the rejected parent and protection from the alienating parent, and the court can assist with this custody issue.

7. **Adolescents' stated custody preferences should control custody decisions.** Adolescents are children, after all. They are vulnerable to outside influence and can be persuaded by an alienator to "tell the courts who you want to live with." This should **never** happen. The court has the ability to enforce a custody order, ensure a child is able to see both parents and not be blamed for the decision.

8. **Children who irrationally reject a parent but thrive in other respects need no intervention.** The cognitive, emotional and behavioral problems that accompany an irrational aversion to a parent, as well as the potential long-term consequences of remaining alienated from a parent is what must be used to evaluate how a child is thriving.

9. **Alienated children are best treated with traditional therapy techniques while living primarily with their alienating parent.** Once again, therapy that has a basis in the historical theories **does not work.** Parental alienation is counterintuitive. Having a child or family attend therapy with a therapist unfamiliar with alienation is worse than no therapy at all. Many therapists who claim to be trained, or

"do reunification therapy" have no background at all and can further deteriorate relationships.

10. **Separating children from their alienating parent is traumatic**. Because a child has had a previously loving relationship with the rejected parent, they are quick to reestablish a relationship with that parent. The trauma is derived from the alienating parent's "warnings and predictions" they will be abused by the alienated parent. Judges can order the alienating parent not to sabotage the reunification and impose sanctions (predetermined) if they do.[18]

What if the judge and lawyers insist on not using the term "parental alienation"?

I admit it is easier for an expert witness to say, "Parental alienation is a well-documented phenomenon and that is the term we use". If you want to circumvent direct confrontation, you can describe in detail what has happened. Tell them what the eight manifestations of PA are, and demonstrate how this is parent alienation. Educating them is imperative.

Recently, I was told about a satirical book on PA, *Parentectomy for Mummies (and Daddies): How To Get Rid of That Useless Other Parent and Improve Your Kids' Lives*. Yes, seriously! It

---

[18] Richard Warshak, "Ten parental alienation fallacies that compromise decisions in court and in therapy," *Professional Psychology: Research and Practice* 46, no.2, (2015): 235–249.

was most likely written by an alienated dad but clearly there is a serious undertone. It is currently available on Amazon.

There *are* deliberate actions an alienator can take to facilitate removing the other parent from their child's lives. What is amazing is that the tactics they use are the same across the board, despite the fact they have not studied for this particular war and think themselves to be unique. It could be lifelong defense mechanisms of personality disordered alienators and/or the influence of uninformed attorneys and the legal system in general.

Whatever it is, it needs to be challenged and changed.

Chapter 9

Trauma And Self-Care For Alienated Parents

"Concentrate your energy and hoard your strength."

– **Sun Tzu**

*F*ollowing a traumatic event, it is a well-documented that the physical manifestations can range from panic attacks and heart attacks to cancer, and everything in between. In the event of parental alienation, the helplessness, depression, and despair that besets a parent who loses their children results in both short-term and long-term suffering.

Parents have shared that when the reality of parental alienation sets in they initially feel psychotic and suicidal.

Reality becomes distorted. A normally sane and functioning parent described how she could actually see half her house in ruin, as if her home had been bombed. In a fugue state, (not drug-induced), she stepped in front of an oncoming bus, which braked in time. This seemed as if it were a dream. She could not say with certainty that she wanted to kill herself. She preferred to stay in bed with the covers over her head. She fell asleep at work, in social situations, and avoided driving because during a freeway traffic jam she dozed off. The pain of losing her children was unbearable.

Parents verbalize not wanting to go on living. They feel life is pointless without their children and make statements such as "this is killing me." Many parents who do kill themselves, do so in the most lethal ways: using a gun, jumping off buildings, overdosing, etc. In the longer run many become terminally ill. I have read many an account of parents who notified their children when they became terminally ill, and more often than not getting no response, or the standard response, "I hope you die soon." It is one of the most horrifying aspects of the alienation. The extent of the hatred an alienated child has towards a formerly beloved parent is incomprehensible although clinically understood. One can only imagine what a child feels when he/she realizes the enormity of what happened. Many alienated children also commit suicide.

Broken heart syndrome

In 1991, medical professionals in Japan recognized Stress-Induced Cardiomyopathy, or "Broken Heart Syndrome". It is a temporary condition, but is severe and painful. The heart muscle is suddenly stunned and so weakened that it can resemble a heart attack. Dr. Scott Sharkey, a research cardiologist at the Minneapolis Heart Institute Foundation states that it is not as benign a condition as originally thought and that "the true mortality rate is only becoming manifest as we have a broader experience" with broken heart syndrome. Johns Hopkins University is now conducting further research of this syndrome.

In an article titled, "No More Poison", leukemia patient, Jim Smith wrote:

> "I have often thought my leukemia could be traced back to a seven-year period when I endured a chronic level of intense stress . . . Though there is little evidence (yet) that stress is a direct cause of leukemia, a growing number of studies connect stress with a reduction in the immune system and possibly the progression of the disease . . ."[19]

---

[19] Jim Smith, "No More Poison," Blood-Cancer.com, July 9, 2019, https://blood-cancer.com/living/toxic-people-relationships/

What can you do to reduce stress?

If you are suffering from stress as a result of PA, the following activities can help:

- meditation
- exercise
- getting enough sleep
- eating well
- reading about parental alienation (you're not alone)
- psychotherapy with a therapist who has studied PA
- joining a support group, on Facebook or in your community
- having a community of supportive friends

But most importantly, getting rid of the source of the stress is what to strive for. However, this is a tall order when it involves your alienated children. Going no-contact with the alienator as much as you can, can cut off that source of distress somewhat. And don't break the cardinal rule, and stalk either the alienator or your children on Facebook. This is hard to do I know, but think of how much worse you will feel when you find out information that hurts you.

One woman was fighting for custody of her children from an alienator for seven years when her body grew a tumor the size of a softball. When she asked her oncologist what caused it, he said constant stress. With the help of an expert witness in alienation, the court awarded her full physical and legal custody with zero visitation for the alienator. Her tumor never came back.

If you cannot endure the pain that alienators and your children bring your way, do not interact with them! Do not let your children abuse you. If they are violent with you, follow through and call the police.

Many parents do not know what to do and how to respond when their children are disrespectful. Respond as their parent, as you did in the past. One parent I have observed confronts her sons immediately whenever they say something outrageous. She does it directly and calmly and this defuses two angry adolescents.

Parents have told their children they cannot see them for a while because of their disrespect and abuse. Set a specified amount of time. This turns the tables on them and gives you some control. With adult children, it is okay to take time-outs.

What works best, is to have boundaries, be unemotional in your contact with them, and be consistent. Alienated children say this response helps to calm them and they associate that with the alienated parent, whereas the home with the alienator is chaotic. Sending a text, calling, emailing, on a regular basis with a loving but calm message helps them. By regular, it could be every day, week, month, or on special occasions.

Some experts say to never give up. But sometimes, it is just too lethal for the alienated parent to stay in a relationship, even with their children. As with the much-quoted example of a parent on an aircraft applying their own oxygen mask before their child's, take care of yourself first, and then help your child.

Alienated children have said that knowing their alienated parent has taken care of themselves and created a life for themselves helps them. Setting boundaries helps with the awful guilt they feel. Letting them know the door is always open, or the "light is always on so you can find your way back home", helps sustain them until they are able to return.

If it makes **you** happy to give children gifts or care packages, do so. Alienated children are often forced to discard them and the gifts are ridiculed by the alienator.

Know that underneath all that rejection, your child loves you, but is powerless to keep a relationship with you in their lives for now.

Let old friendships and family members (flying monkeys) go if they do not understand and are hurtful to you. You will make other friends. Avoid toxic people, but don't isolate forever. Go out. Join groups—Facebook has an enormous number of groups for alienated parents. Join the ones you feel are the best for you. You can find lots of support on this forum.

Go to psychotherapy with a therapist who is trained in parental alienation dynamics. There are support groups in many States, some of them free, as well as phone-in and Meetup groups you can participate in. The following are a selection of PA professionals and organizations that offer support. The information listed is correct at the time of publication, but please check their websites or phone ahead to confirm current services and contacts.

Family Access—Fighting for Children's Rights holds monthly lectures by experts who are attorneys, psychologists, and psychotherapists. Their website lists upcoming events, informative videos, and contact information for many experts. President, Elaine Cobb can be contacted directly, and she endeavors to talk to everyone who calls her. PAS-I has referrals listed by State, and Joan Kloth-Zanard is also available to talk to alienated parents. ISNAF in Los Angeles, CA, has call-in groups twice a month and Dr. Linda Gunsberg in New York City also has a support group for alienated parents once a month. Howie Dennison from Ohio has a website with a plethora of information about parental alienation. I also provide a free support group for alienated parents in Los Angeles the second Sunday of each month.

If you want to be part of something bigger, get involved with a PA group that is attempting to change the law. You can also join or start a group that provides help to other alienated parents or start a blog about what you have learned that would be of assistance to others.

Educate yourself and others. In the ten years I have known about alienation, it has become more widely known and prominent in many ways. The number of books, articles, conferences, Facebook groups, and support in the community has grown exponentially. It is encouraging. But we still have work to do. You can be part of the solution. There are films, documentaries, network shows, and more, that you can show to others. Try anything and everything. It is healing.

Travel if you like to do that. Traveling alone can be a great experience and help you reach a new level of independence and enjoyment.

Have a favorite podcast, audiobook, radio program, book, or album, ready for the times when you start obsessing about the whole alienating situation. Most parents report they cannot sleep through the night. Stopping your mind from going around and around and interfering with the negative cycle, can help your general state of mind.

If you are having a day where you are so depressed and getting out of bed is too much of an effort, give in to it. Get everything you need to eat and drink for the day, turn on the TV, get back under the covers and binge-watch for the whole day. You will most likely feel better the next day and be able to go about your business.

However, if you are feeling a sense of hopelessness most days that you are unable to shake, and you are concerned you are depressed, talk to a health professional immediately. Don't feel like you have to push through alone, help is always available.

When exiting the relationship, is grieving normal?

Grieving the relationship is not only normal, it's a healthy process to experience the following:

- Stage 1: Feeling dumbfounded, shocked inert, immobile, in pain
- Stage 2: Feeling enraged, indignant, rebellious, and hateful
- Stage 3: Acceptance, tears
- Stage 4: Learning to forgive, healing

Permanent grieving is the continuation of the abuse. It is by moving on that the abuser is defeated, and their importance in one's life is minimized. Loving and trusting anew heals the abuse that was perpetrated by the narcissist. Forgiving is not forgetting and remembering is not re-experiencing necessarily.

Knowing one's own part in the narcissistic dance will allow recognition of any future narcissistic relationship. Realizing when one is being love bombed, or gaslighted, or manipulated in other ways can send you running in the opposite direction. It is helpful to continually assess the relationships in your life: friends, partners, family, business partners. A common past is not sufficient to sustain a relationship. Human relationships are a constant test of allegiance and empathy, and if those qualities are not present, they can be found in a new relationship, friendship, or career.

Can you stay friends with the former partner/narcissist?

Narcissists are only friendly when:

- they need something
- they feel threatened

- they feel infused with a narcissistic supply and feel magnanimous (e.g. they just won the Nobel Peace Prize!)

For your own peace of mind, go "no-contact". Narcissists envy success, property, your character, education, ideas, and children. Almost anything can trigger biting, acerbic envy. Keep your happiness to yourself. It is a narcissistic injury to see someone else happy when their importance in your life is reduced. You should, after all, be unhappy. They are angry that you are no longer under their control.

The narcissist will admit to "pain and shame", appearing vulnerable, to gain a supply of empathy from others. It is a manipulative ploy. Anything you do will somehow be used against you, so it is wise to keep your distance. A "healed" narcissist is a contradiction in terms. They damage and hurt others naturally, reflexively. They are aware of what they do, but do not care.

Chapter 10

Treatment Available For Alienated Parents And Their Children

"All men can see these tactics by which I conquer, but what none can see is the strategy out of which victory is evolved."

– **Sun Tzu**

*E*nglish psychologist Dr. Ludwig Lowenstein was one of the pioneers in the theory of parental alienation. He wrote a book and over a hundred articles on the topic of PA, which included recommendations on how to treat alienated parents and children. He was also subjected to character assassination and his work was unfairly denigrated by those who wish to deny parental alienation exists.

Throughout the course of his work, Dr. Lowenstein observed the following behaviors in alienated children:

- anger
- loss of impulse control in conduct
- loss of self-confidence and self-esteem
- clinging and separation anxiety
- developing fears and phobias
- depression and suicidal ideation
- sleep disorders
- eating disorders
- educational problems
- enuresis and encopresis (lack of bowel control in young children)
- drug abuse and self-destructive behavior
- obsessive-compulsive behavior
- anxiety and panic attacks
- damaged sexual identity
- poor peer relationships
- excessive feelings of guilt

Dr. Lowenstein's work predated Dr. Richard Gardner's work, and he recommended treatment upon which current approaches are based. The primary aspect of reunification is partnering with and supporting the alienated parent. Because the rejected parent has been made so powerless by the alienator, their children, the courts etc., the only real approach is to re-empower the alienated parent. The therapist becomes the "bad guy", confronting and dealing with false allegations and behavior in the children, while the alienated parent takes the role of the "good guy".

The four steps that successful reunification treatment is based upon are outlined below:

1. **Dealing with the hatred developed**

   The indoctrination by the alienated parent which has caused hatred and paranoia in the alienated child must be addressed first and foremost. This is done through rational and logical arguments by the therapist. The real reason for the false beliefs must be attended to and labeled as hearsay or the opinion of others, not based in fact.

2. **The child identifying with the alienated parent**

   Children do not remember a former relationship with the alienated parent. Using photographs, letters, cards, stories, videos and other mementos helps dispel the indoctrinated belief that they had no relationship with that parent. The only course of action for the therapist **is to side with the alienated parent.** Alienated children have been given an inordinate amount of power over the alienated parent. This is perpetrated by the legal system, family, the alienator, and most especially therapists. "Disempowering the child" and once more establishing the parent as an authority has to happen for the therapy to be successful. It is the only way for healing to take place.

3. **Treating the alienator**

   Alienators know exactly what they are doing but deny they are programming their children. The **only** way to deal with an alienator is to get the court to

125

sanction them should they sabotage treatment. It is up to the judge to:

- prepare the alienator for the treatment
- order treatment for the alienator and have it documented by an alienation therapist
- monitor the alienator through the behavior of the child and use sanctions if the alienating parent does not cooperate, to the point of losing custody of the child

4. **Monitoring the effects of treatment against alienation**

   The children will exhibit the alienator's behavior, and if it has changed, they will demonstrate that in regard to their behavior toward the rejected parent. If they are still displaying alienating behavior, returning to court and reporting it to the judge is the best approach. If the alienator can be dealt with in mediation, that can be an option.

Linda Gottlieb runs an intensive four-day reunification program for families called Turning Points, which encompasses many of Dr. Lowenstein principles and has a 99 percent success rate. The program aims to reconnect the alienated child and parent, dispel the lies surrounding the alienated parent, and cement the progress and reconciliation with the child. Gottlieb joins the family for meals and attends activities with them to observe real-life situations. She also attends court as an expert witness, asking the judge for a ninety-day transfer of custody to allow the child to bond with their alienated parent. Before the reunification program commences, she speaks briefly with the alienator, to assure them the children will be safe throughout the program.

My own family reconciliation program is based on the successful Turning Points model. I spend three days working closely with the alienated parent and children. I also encourage them to participate in an outing or trip before the fourth day, so we can observe and deal with any issues that may have arisen. They return for the fourth day to cement progress and deal with any issues that arose during the trip. As part of the intervention, I follow up once a month for a year with parents to find out how the relationship is progressing, and if there are any problems, we meet again.

Like Gottlieb, I insist on a ninety-day transfer of custody to the alienated parent to ensure success. However, if that is not an option (as in DCFS cases), I will meet with the parent and children once a week for two hours, but only with the support of the judge, and sanctions for the alienator. With adult children, meeting two to three hours every two weeks can be managed, with tasks to be done in between meetings. A contract with the adult children is also required to be signed and returned as part of the treatment.

A sixteen-year-old boy was ordered into weekly reunification therapy by the judge. He was sullen and uncooperative at first, and I had to pull out all my skills, plus threatening to write to the judge if he did not cooperate. Finally, after many months of meeting two hours a week, and realizing the meetings were not going to stop, he capitulated and began calling his dad during the week (a homework assignment to demonstrate he was not against reunification). His dad invited him to go on a camping trip with his new family. This appealed to him. Upon returning from the trip, they all came to the session and talked about how wonderful it was, the smaller children loving having a big brother and sitting on his lap. It has been five months since I have seen them, the reunification is holding, and the formerly alienated son is spending time at his father's house, even bringing his formerly alienated sister with him. She is 20 years old and had successfully avoided reunification therapy with her father while she was still in the court system.

Family Bridges is another parental alienation program developed by Dr. Richard Warshak. He is located in Texas, but there are programs operating under that name in California and other areas.

There are additional treatment programs available, some of which are residential, and exist in different states. Specific programs can be recommended by treating alienation therapists, or check the websites of the main experts in PA as they will often list the therapists they recommend there. You can also try a google search for "Parental Alienation Treatment", or "PA Therapist." Be sure to read all their reviews thoroughly, as (once again) many therapists advertise themselves as parental alienation therapists, but they have not actually completed any specific training in PA. Some claim to be an "expert" because they have read a few articles or a book on the subject. Let's be clear—this does not qualify them to diagnose or treat parental alienation.

An investigation of the different treatment programs would be a valuable and much needed undertaking. Parental alienation reunification therapy is a drawing card for psychotherapists these days, so more and more are listing it on their "specialization areas", which are usually many. Then, when they register as a PA therapist with the court and get referrals, they proceed to use the usual Family Systems model honoring the child's word over the parent who is already disempowered. As mentioned throughout this book, this NEVER works, and the therapist is simply doing the job of the alienator. Going to such a therapist is worse than not going to a therapist at all. If you are seeking a reunification program or therapist, always take the time to seek out those who are genuinely knowledgeable and experienced in working with parental alienation.

Chapter 11

What's Next? Creating Your New Normal

"We may distinguish six kinds of terrain, to wit: accessible ground, entangling ground, temporizing ground, narrow passes, precipitous heights, and positions of great distance from the enemy."

– Sun Tzu

*O*nce reconciliation therapy is over, or your child has reappeared in your life, it will not necessarily be smooth sailing. If your children are young, it is important to have them in your life and spend time with them. When a parent is not present in a child's life, that absence will be the fertile soil for the extreme hatred toward an alienated parent to grow. When there is constant contact, the reality of the

131

loving parent/child bond is able to remain intact, and the false accusations and expressed hostility can be addressed in a timely fashion.

Even after reconciliation therapy, if the alienating parent continues with the attacks and accusations towards the alienated parent, the child will act out as they did before. However, with constant contact, a positive relationship can develop with the alienated parent and the child can begin to understand the way in which the alienation is taking place and recognize the lies.

With adult children, parents report that the road to reconciliation is rocky. Adult children will appear to have reconciled, and then some unknown occurrence will cause a regression back into the alienation, which has again been provoked by the alienator. Sometime later, there will be another contact and reconciliation, and that fails too. This has been reported to go on for a few years before there is a complete reunion. At times it will appear the relationship with the adult child is back to the loving parent/child relationship that existed before the split, and then comes a declaration that there can never be a parent/child relationship again. One can only imagine what the threatened alienator is claiming to keep the bonds permanently severed!

Dr. Amy Baker recommends a different approach to reconciling with an adult child. She helps a parent develop a letter that lists all the situations which the parent knows the child was hurt, and asks for forgiveness and contact with the child. Dr. Joshua Coleman also recommends this approach, and the follow up therapy is to listen to the child and apologize. Ryan Thomas, a formerly alienated child, helps parents write to their children, keeping them as the main focus and not mentioning the parent's feelings so that the child doesn't interpret communications to be all about the parent's needs. The above is paraphrased, and taken from what I have heard and interpreted (liberally) Dr. Baker, Dr. Coleman, and Ryan Thomas to have said.

Letting your child know that no matter what, you will love them and the door is always open to them is important. What is more important is that when you contact them, express an interest in them. Alienated children often interpret, "I love you and miss you" to be self-serving for the rejected parent. The turmoil and heartache is once again fresh with the alienated parent. You can see how important it is to have a full life, independent of your alienated children, so the comings and goings are easier to cope with.

Keep in mind that the damage the child has suffered is overriding whatever is occurring in the back and forth reconnections. You have suffered greatly too. Hopefully, eventually, your child will realize the pathology of the situation and not want to leave again.

Many parents ask me "When can **I** show my child the court papers or tell them what **really** happened?" The short answer to that question, is "NEVER! DON'T DO IT!" Your child has heard ad nauseam, "what really happened" from the alienator. Stay away from the subject, and as hard as it is, **do not** bad mouth their other parent. I have observed adult and younger children visibly flinch when the alienated parent starts to blame the alienator. The child needs to come to the realization themselves. The parent can objectively give correct information, for example, telling the child they did indeed pay child support in the amount of …… a month. It is easier and preferable in reconciliation therapy for the therapist to dispel a belief, false accusation, or misinformation fed to them by the alienating parent and be the "bad guy."

Linda Gottlieb has talked about the amazing transformation that takes place between parent and child when they are able to communicate with one another again. It is where the healing takes place. It is the therapist's work to bring the relationship to this place. I have myself witnessed the excitement in the child, as well as the vulnerability and acceptance of the alienated parent. From this point, it does not take many hours before the parent and child are conversing lovingly with one another once again.

Keep in mind what was said before: be the haven of sanity for your child. Be a consistent, loving, calm presence. Do not ask too much. That means, understand what their experience is and keep your emotions in check as much as possible.

Having your own life will play a big part in this. Your child will be able to observe that they are not your life (although they may be) and feel relief that they can be themselves with you. It will fortify your relationship with them and they will want to get to know you as well. An alienated child related how relieved she was each time she contacted her mother, as she heard positive stories and remarks. She said it sounded so "calm and sane" at her mother's house. This was juxtaposed with the chaos and negativity she experienced with the alienator.

Chapter 12

Changing The Law

"Sometimes we need to win small battles in order to win the war."

-Sun Tzu

The phenomenon of parent alienation exists worldwide, and it is not just an American conceptualization writes Ashish Joshi in the book *Parental Alienation, Science and the Law, 2020*. Despite the fact it is known by different names in some countries, there is recognition across the board that children (adult children as well) will alienate a parent when they are manipulated by the other parent to hold "false and distorted thoughts and feelings about the rejected parent".[20]

---

[20] Desmosthenes Lorandos and William Bernet, *Parental Alienation – Science and Law* (Springfield: Charles C Thomas Publisher, 2020).

At the time of writing, there are the three countries that have laws against parental alienation in place: Brazil, Mexico, and Denmark. I have included the laws in Appendix A for your perusal and to use as a resource in the event you have the opportunity to pursue changes to the law in your own country or state. In my opinion, there are three important pieces to include in any legislation:

1. Parental alienation is psychological child abuse
2. There has to be mandatory education for professions, including judges, lawyers, court personnel, mediators, and all the psychological professions, including DCFS caseworkers
3. Mandatory reporting, which should include the same reporters found in the Child Abuse Law.

I have worked with many alienated parents. It is rewarding to see them work through the initial stage and feel empowered to make choices about their situation. Once the parent is reconciled with their children, they want to enjoy that time and not continue to be involved in parental alienation. This is also rewarding. However, there are also many alienated parents and grandparents who get involved with campaigning to change the laws and attitudes around PA. For example, the mother of Michelle Neurauter, has become involved in changing the law to make parental alienation child abuse and therefore a crime.

THE HAGUE CONVENTION

This is the International Court which passed a law in 1980 called "The Civil Aspects of International Child Abuse". It states that if a country which was part of the Convention decides on custody of a child or children, the **new country** does not have the right to retry custody. The "new" country has to return the children to the country of "habitual residence." This includes visitation. It means that if one parent has visitation rights and the other parent kidnaps the children to another country, they have to return with the children so that visitation can continue. The law exists to protect the child's relationship with both parents. Since it is a criminal act to kidnap a child, even one's own, the parent can be charged criminally and go to jail.[21]

In the US, there are currently laws in all 50 States against kidnapping one's own children. It is considered unacceptable. Specifically, the laws address the sudden, secretive taking of children by one parent without the knowledge of the other parent. Even when the custodial parent kidnaps the children it is considered a crime.

There are presently no laws against parental alienation in the US. There are Penal Codes in each state, which means they are criminal acts when committed. For example:

---

[21] Richard A. Gardner, Richard S. Sauber and Desmosthenes Lorandos, *The International Handbook of Parental Alienation Syndrome* (Springfield: Charles C Thomas, 2006).

California Penal Code Section 278.5: Child Abduction by Depriving Right to Custody or Visitation.

It generally applies if one individual who has legal custody of a child unlawfully deprives another person who has also has custody of that minor, or has visitation rights.

The parent who withholds the child may face charges for:

- Taking, keeping, concealing, withholding or enticing away a minor under the age of 18
- To maliciously deprive one of the minor's legal custodian the right to visitation **(even if the minor child consented and wanted to stay with them)**
- Individuals do not have the right to use force to keep, take or conceal a minor

In most cases, divorcing parents are given rules about custody. These rules include which parent should have legal custody of the minor children at any given moment. Individuals who intentionally and maliciously violate these rules can be charged under PC 278.5.

Penalties

Depriving right to custody or visitation as a consequence of withholding the child penalties are outlined below.

Misdemeanor violations of 278.5:

- Fines of up to $1,000.00 per child
- Jail time of up to one year per child

Felony 278.5 violations:

- Fines of up to $10,000.00 per child
- Jail time of up to three years

Alienators get around this by saying the children are afraid they will be abused by the other parent (coaching the children to say this), and beginning legal proceedings to "protect" the children.

Parents who have called the police when they are unable to get court ordered custody time with their children have been told it is a civil matter and to go back to Family Court to get the judge to order on this issue. In spite of the fact that judges hate to make children go with parents the child is claiming abused them, they say the police has to enforce a criminal violation. There seems to be no resolution in this respect. Yet.

States working to change the child abuse law to include parental alienation

In Los Angeles, California, there is an ongoing attempt to change the Child Abuse Law to include *Psychological Abuse of children (parental alienation), and Mandatory Training and Reporting of Parent/Child Alienation Abuse for Professionals.*

It is hoped that introducing it as an Amendment to the Child Abuse Law would make it easier to pass. In 2018, it made it through two committees, but not the Appropriations Committee. In 2019, the senator declined to sponsor it.

GETTING A BILL PASSED INTO LAW: OVERVIEW OF LEGISLATIVE PROCESS

The process of government by which bills are considered and laws enacted is commonly referred to as the legislative process. To provide an overview of how this works, below is a description of the legislative process in the State of California, but this may vary from state to state.

The California State Legislature is made up of two houses: the Senate and the Assembly. There are forty senators and eighty assembly members representing the people of the State of California. The legislature has a legislative calendar containing important dates of activities during its two-year session.

The steps of the legislative process are described below:

Idea: All legislation begins as an idea or concept. Ideas and concepts can come from a variety of sources. The process begins when a senator or assembly member decides to author a bill.

The Author: A legislator sends the idea for the bill to the Legislative Counsel where it is drafted into the actual bill. The draft of the bill is returned to the legislator for introduction. If the author is a senator, the bill is introduced in the Senate. If the author is an assembly member, the bill is introduced in the Assembly.

First reading/introduction: A bill is introduced or read the first time when the bill number, the name of the author, and the descriptive title of the bill is read on the floor of the house. The bill is then sent to the Office of State Printing. No bill may be acted upon until thirty days has passed from the date of its introduction.

Committee hearings: The bill then goes to the rules committee of the house of origin where it is assigned to the appropriate policy committee for its first hearing. Bills are assigned to policy committees according to subject area of the bill. For example, a Senate bill dealing with health care facilities would first be assigned to the Senate Health and Human Services Committee for policy review. Bills that require the expenditure of funds must also be heard in the fiscal committees: Senate Appropriations or Assembly Appropriations. Each house has a number of policy committees and a fiscal committee. Each committee is made up of a specified number of senators or assembly members.

During the committee hearing the author presents the bill to the committee and testimony can be heard in support of or opposition to the bill. The committee then votes by passing the bill, passing the bill as amended, or defeating the bill. Bills can be amended several times. Letters of support or opposition are important and should be mailed to the author and committee members before the bill is scheduled to be heard in committee. It takes a majority vote of the full committee membership for a bill to be passed by the committee.

Each house maintains a schedule of legislative committee hearings. Prior to a bill's hearing, a bill analysis is prepared that explains current law, what the bill is intended to do, and some background information. Typically the analysis also lists organizations that support or oppose the bill.

Second and third reading: Bills passed by committees are read a second time on the floor in the house of origin and then assigned to third reading. Bill analyses are also prepared prior to the third reading. When a bill is read the third time it is explained by the author, discussed by the members and voted on by a roll call vote. Bills that require an appropriation or that take effect immediately, generally require twenty-seven votes in the Senate and fifty-four votes in the Assembly to be passed. Other bills generally require twenty-one votes in the Senate and forty-one votes in the Assembly. If a bill is defeated, the member may seek reconsideration and another vote.

Repeat process in the other house: Once the bill has been approved by the house of origin it proceeds to the other house where the procedure is repeated.

Resolution of differences: If a bill is amended in the second house, it must go back to the house of origin for concurrence, which is agreement on the amendments. If agreement cannot be reached, the bill is referred to a two house conference committee to resolve differences. Three members of the committee are from the Senate and three are from the Assembly. If a compromise is reached, the bill is returned to both houses for a vote.

Governor: If both houses approve a bill, it then goes to the governor. The governor has three choices—they can sign the bill into law, allow it to become law without his or her signature, or veto it. A governor's veto can be overridden by a two-thirds vote in both houses. Most bills go into effect on the first day of January of the next year. Urgency measures take effect immediately after they are signed or allowed to become law without signature.

California Law: Bills that are passed by the legislature and approved by the governor are assigned a chapter number by the Secretary of State. These Chaptered Bills (also referred to as Statutes of the year they were enacted) then become part of the California Codes. The California Codes are a comprehensive collection of laws grouped by subject matter.

The California Constitution sets forth the fundamental laws by which the State of California is governed. All amendments to the Constitution come about as a result of constitutional amendments presented to the people for their approval.[22]

[22] "Overview of the Legislative Process," Official California Legislative Information, accessed September 27, 2020, http://www.leginfo.ca.gov/bil2lawx.html.

There is a psychological adage that says: *"Stateways make folkways."*

What this means is that once a law is enacted, it becomes a common way of life, just as the Child Abuse Law has. Most people know there are laws against committing child abuse, that professionals in helping professions— teachers, therapists, and law personnel, amongst others— are "Mandated Reporters". They are obligated to report child abuse when they become aware of it (and can be prosecuted if they do not). It is up to the police, sheriffs, and Department of Child and Family Services to investigate the report further.

Most alienated parents are all too familiar with the process as they are most often the target of false child abuse accusations and constant harassment in the form of police visits.

However, as seen from those countries who have enacted law to combat parental alienation, including parent/child alienation in the child abuse law is imperative. This problem will not be reduced or eliminated until alienators understand it is child abuse and they will be held accountable by the law for abusing their children by eliminating a beloved parent from their children's lives.

Getting legislation passed requires a committed legislator. Finding one who can dedicate themselves to getting a bill passed is difficult. Finding a legislator who is also an alienated parent would be ideal. Additionally, getting associations to sponsor the bill is part of the leg work. The American Society of Pediatricians recognizes parental alienation, for example, so that would be a good organization to approach. In California, the Board of Behavioral Sciences initially supported legislation but then backed out because they were concerned about giving their licensees (social workers and therapists) "more material to study" as they were already overloaded. This does not appear to be a good excuse to me as it would be part of the child abuse coursework.

Something else legislators are concerned about is where the money would come from to enact the legislation. They require a preamble that would include a plan to obtain any money to support the legislation. Presumably, these funds would come from the associations sponsoring the legislation, as well as interested parents.

Chapter 13

Why Do We Choose An Alienator With Whom To Partner And Have Children?

"Using order to deal with the disorderly, using calm to deal with the clamorous, is mastering the heart."
–Sun Tzu

*T*his question is the one that is asked often, and in hindsight. Alienated parents can often identify signs before they married and had children. Some were even warned by others to not marry the alienator-to-be. Yet invariably, warning signs are ignored.

When alienated parents are asked why they ignored all warnings, they generally answer they thought their partner "just needed to be loved", or "no one else really understands him or her". Their nurturing tendencies are aroused by the future spouse, who is co-dependent, as is the alienated parent.

In the following explanation, borderline personality disorder (BPD) and narcissistic personality disorder (NPD) is used to describe symptoms, but they can be applied to other personality disorders as well.

The borderline/narcissistic/sociopathic/and psychopathic personality disorders are all capable of "love bombing", or charming and seducing the target. Everyone is a potential target, including others with personality disorders. Their only concern is whether or not the potential partner is willing and able to provide narcissistic "supplies."

Sam Vaknin, author of the *Malignant Self-Love*, and several other books on the subject, states narcissists are interested in "the three S's":

- sex
- servitude
- supply (meeting their needs emotionally, physically, sexually)[23]

Many people are taken aback by these personality disorders. They feel uncomfortable by their lack of boundaries.

---

[23] Sam Vaknin, *Malignant Self-Love: Narcissism Revealed* (Skopje: Narcissus, 2001).

"Something" is missing, despite their ability to simulate "normal." Since the target was most likely raised in a family with a similar lack of boundaries and lack of self, this feels familiar to them. The narcissist is disdainful of small talk and provides an intensity to an initial conversation thereby attracting, or conversely repulsing in the target. This gives them information about who is likely to be a reliable source of supply, meaning servitude and sex.

They use the following manipulations, progressively:

Love bombing: Endless questions, texts, intended to charm and allege one's love, which blocks the ability to think critically about the situation. The promises: "I'll never hurt you", the seduction: "you are my soulmate", "you are beautiful, wonderful", "I only feel comfortable being with you", appeal to the target's own narcissism. Everyone needs a modicum of healthy narcissism. Feeling adored and invaluable creates the high one experiences when infatuated and excited about another person.

Shared fantasy: This becomes the element that cements the relationship. It involves who the partners are, what their plans are, sex, children, homes, careers, etc.

A couple I knew, both narcissists, were enamored of one another. He was a successful executive in the entertainment business and she came from an old family in the business. They were both missing what the other wanted. Their egos did not allow them to live in the same house, so they saw one another on weekends, rekindling their grandiose union.

All their money and status did not allow anyone else in their lives who disagreed with them or did not admire them. The children from one of their former marriage's became the victims.

Grooming: The partner receives approval and love when they provide what the narcissist wants, and disapproval and withdrawal when they do not.

Gaslighting: Lies about motivation and situations which may reveal their true inability to be intimate and loving.

There was a famous movie which perfectly described this phenomenon. A husband reduced the brightness of the lights in the home a slight amount every day. He told his wife she was "imagining things" when she complained about not being able to see clearly. A metaphor for the experience of being in a relationship with a personality disorder.

Brainwashing: Alienated parents describe how they had a positive relationship with their adult child until they married. The daughter/son-in-law begins to brainwash them against their parents and deny them relationships with the grandchildren because they judge them to be undeserving, abusive, etc. The adult child begins to believe the spouse and alienates his/her parents, unable to sustain their own reality.

Isolating: Targets are isolated from friends and family and can only have a relationship with the partner. A woman described how she had to fight for her relationships with her friends, who were later co-opted, lied to and turned against her by her husband. This was his way of punishing her for wanting other relationships and controlling the relationships himself.

There are many ways people with personality disorders manipulate their significant others. In addition to the above, they create an intense attachment to themselves, habituate the target into providing them sustenance, dismantling their morality and becoming their "partners in crime", demanding a mindlessness in their partner to create an allegiance and dependency, forming an external locus of control (the target no longer trusts their internal instincts) and becoming their "master" in all areas. For example, one spouse ended all sentences with "you know" or "don't you agree?". He/she defers to the partner constantly, becoming a shell of themselves.

In a "normal relationship", once the infatuation stage has worn itself out, intimacy develops. A narcissist has zero interest in intimacy. When there is a mutual interest in intimacy, both of the couple's needs are met. The desire of the partner to have their needs met as well, arouses rage and feelings of betrayal. The unspoken initial contract is that the partner agrees to provide sex, service and narcissistic supplies, which included continued adoration and idealization. At this point, if the target is steadfast in their refusal to supply the demands, the union will begin to disintegrate.

An example would be when the narcissist is asked to share in the housework, cooking, child-care and even financial necessities, they may initially agree to cooperate, but will not follow through. They become resentful and punishing toward their partner. They lose interest and begin to look elsewhere for other forms of idealization, and this can include their children. Sex is dispensable because they have to meet the other's needs. (One can see the potential here for sexual abuse). But children can provide narcissistic supplies and service, idealization and adoration.

A marriage can survive this if the spouse turns away and attempts to get their needs met by others, or through activities, career, and even extramarital sex. It is more satisfactory to the narcissist if the partner is threatened by the loss of the relationship and returns to being the provider. This in a practical sense means the victim gives over control to the narcissist and the cycle continues.

Chapter 14

PARTNER'S PERSPECTIVE: Helping The Alienated Parent You Love

"He will win whose army is animated by the same spirit throughout all its ranks."

— **Sun Tzu**

*T*his chapter was provided by Melanie Funes, Ph.D., whose partner is alienated from his two sons. The advice is intended to help the new partners of alienated parents who frequently feel helpless and do not know what their role is and how they can help their partner.

LESSON 1: UNDERSTAND YOUR ROLE

You didn't break it. You cannot fix it. Even if you could (which you can't) it is not yours to fix. Deal with your anger—put it in its proper place—then move on to a more productive frame of reference against the alienating parent, against the children, and against your partner.

Yes, your partner—I was surprised to find myself so angry at him for choosing the mother of his children so poorly, for bringing a past to our relationship that permeated negatively into so many aspects of our life in the present. This is unproductive and it serves only to inflict further pain on an already wounded soul. It also gives the alienating parent one more turn of the knife in your partner's back—do not give them that power.

Feel it, explore it, then don't let your anger at his younger self cloud your judgment about who he is today.

Be kind—really kind—to yourself, to your partner, and to the children (even in your mind, when you don't have contact with them). They are walking pieces of your partner, and your partner loves them beyond belief no matter all the horrible things they've said and done. Your partner wants to know you love them too.

Choose the battles you bring to your partner, addressing the most important things and letting the rest go. You may not know how to make things better, but you know which buttons to push to make things worse. Don't do that. Be sensitive to your partner's limited emotional bandwidth at times. This person is in a flight to save their children and every part of their being is wrapped up in that. If your problem can wait then save it for another day. Take care of yourself so you can live to fight another day.

LESSON 2: REMIND THEM THEY ARE WORTHY OF LOVE

The Problem
- Your partner is being abused by the alienating parent and children
- They are constantly being told and shown, in incredibly cruel ways, that they are not worthy of love and respect
- How they are being treated may make them question whether they are worthy of good things
- If they start to believe the hateful messages the alienating parent is using the children to deliver— *you've been abandoned, you're unwanted, you're unloved, you're an awful person*—their self-worth will plummet
- Over time this 'undeserving' mindset spreads into other aspects of their life and other areas start to suffer—a vicious cycle, self-fulfilling prophecy
- As their confidence is slowly eroded, they can become insecure and defensive—this is not a mindset that will help them win the war they are fighting to save their children

Tangible things you can do to protect and nurture their self-worth

Prime them to change their mindset from a fixed mindset to one of growth. There is a strong link between holding a growth mindset and rebounding from failure. If your partner is anything like mine, saying, "You're a great dad" tends to fall on deaf ears. I can almost hear the obnoxious voices in his head countering me and saying, "How would she know? You're not her dad" or "If you were a great dad your kids wouldn't hate you so much, they wouldn't want you dead."

Instead, I found that praising all the hard work and effort he puts into being a great dad gets heard. It's hard to argue against facts. I remind him that he calls his sons every day at 7:45pm, even though they don't answer and don't call him back, which demonstrates that he's always there for them. That he is being a great dad because he's sending them that message even though it breaks his heart every time. I also remind him of the war he is waging on parental alienation in court, hiring experts to advise him, his countless hours of research, etc. He is being a great dad because he's fighting to protect his sons even as they fight to erase him.

By helping your partner to practice growth mindset thinking and behavior, it encourages self-improvement. This is especially important when everything they've ever said and done is being scrutinized in different ways by the alienating parent, their children, friends and family, attorneys, custody evaluators, therapists, etc.

Talk about how no one is perfect, we all make mistakes, and hindsight is 20/20—none of this "caused" the children's complete rejection of your partner as a parent. Instead of dwelling on the past, which cannot be changed, use this as an opportunity to admit past mistakes, learn from them, and practice new parenting approaches so you have more tools to use when the children return. Read parenting blogs, books, etc. to gain insight and knowledge, and try out new communication styles and practice them together.

Show your partner, through your actions, that they are worthy of your time and effort. For example, my partner works a very early shift to be back home before his sons get released from school. He is usually up by three o'clock in the morning, makes breakfast, and sits alone at the kitchen table while everyone else sleeps. I should mention, he is not the happiest camper when he wakes up. I have a sense he was one of those babies that woke up cranky every day and from every nap. I on the other hand, tend to bounce out of bed with a "Good morning world! It's a fresh new day!" attitude.

When his sons refused to come home after a weekend with their mother, and the complete contact refusal started, those mornings sitting alone at breakfast took on a new weight for him.

I started getting up when he did. While he was getting ready, I would make breakfast, then sit with him while he ate.

At first, he thought I was crazy and said as much. Over time it's become something to look forward to ("What will she make today?") and a new way to start the day together.

Another example was to introduce a regular exercise routine. I organized our workouts and made us get through them (during the pandemic!).

LESSON 3: BRING THE CHEER—CELEBRATE HOLIDAYS AND SPECIAL DAYS

The Problem
- They will not want to celebrate
- They will want to hide in a hole away from everyone and pretend the day isn't actually happening without their children
- Holidays and special days will seem insurmountable and be extra heart breaking

There is nothing quite like your partner's children refusing to see him or talk to him on Father's Day. My thoughtful sister-in-law acknowledged my partner on Father's Day which cheered him up.

Tangible things you can do to celebrate your partner

Remind them that there are things worth celebrating even if the children aren't there. My partner is a father—even when his children are not with him—and he is worth celebrating. Change the narrative from, "If the kids were here, we could

. . . but they won't be so we shouldn't" to "I wish the kids could've been here to enjoy this with us."

LESSON 4: EDUCATING THEMSELVES

The Problem
- They will not have the heart at times to become their own expert (e.g., read the book, listen to the talk, etc.). The subject matter is too close to home, too painful
- The more they learn the more depressing they realize the potential outcome could be

Tangible things you can do to become the expert

Sift through the research and provide your partner with insights and relevant information in manageable doses. Join support groups (e.g., ISNAF, PASG) to further your support network and understanding.

Bring them stories depending on where they are emotionally. I spent a lot of time trying to find stories with happy endings, so it wasn't always doom and gloom. When you do find these stories, reach out to people who have gone through similar journeys to remind him he is not in this alone.

Find and vet experts (in preparation for court, therapy, etc.). I put together binders and binders of historic court documents, findings letters from DCFS, and emails categorized by subject (making certain points). The point is to make it easy to find information when you need it—when DCFS shows up at their door (again, for the tenth time!), when they have to explain the history to yet another therapist or evaluator, etc.

Pull together data and present it in new ways to tell their story (e.g., we spent a lot of time analyzing school performance. It turned out the data showed nicely what we already knew, that after visits with their mother homework wasn't getting turned in, performance on tests was lower, etc.).

LESSON 5: EDUCATE FAMILY AND FRIENDS— RUN INTERFERENCE

The Problem

Your partner is being doubly abused by the alienating parent—first through the children and then inadvertently through well-meaning family/friends.

The questions and comments your partner will get from well-intentioned family/friends can be very insensitive, for example:

- "Why do they hate you so much?"
- "They seem so angry. It must be about something you've done."
- "Have you tried…?"
- "Maybe if you did…"

- "Maybe if you weren't…"
- "If my kids did that I would…"
- "Eh, they'll grow out of it eventually"
- "Why don't you just let them stay with their mom if that's where they want to be?"

Defending themselves directly is pointless as they won't have the energy to educate each person, so their defense won't make sense or won't be believed (parental alienation is counterintuitive). This only adds more fuel to the gossip mill. It's also often too painful to discuss with everyone who asks and your partner won't want to keep a conversation about this issue going.

Tangible things you can do to educate and run interference

Identify the key family members and educate them—then rally the troops when needed. Step in if/when you hear a conversation go down this road. Give your partner time to retreat, change the subject, etc. Remind family and friends that no matter how upset, sad, depressed, or angry they feel about the alienation, it pales in comparison to what your partner is going through. They need to look elsewhere for support (e.g., a good therapist). If they don't understand that and keep looking to you and your partner for support to help them through their feelings, then create some distance so you can focus your energy on helping your partner.

An example of this was a female family member who during Father's Day focused solely on how badly she was missing the children, how sad she was, how tragic the situation was for her, how this was happening to her, going so far as to say, "I can't believe she (the alienating parent) is doing this to me" (what?!). My partner wasn't mentioned once. Perspective is everything.

As Colombian soccer player, Andres Escobar, stated, "See you soon, because life does not end here."

Conclusion

"Victory comes in finding opportunities in problems."

— **Sun Tzu**

*I*t is my sincere hope that the reader will find this book to be a useful guide. I wrote it because I find myself often repeating the information in the book to people who seek my help.

The majority of the information on parental alienation is translatable globally, however, no matter where you live, I suggest you seek local advice on all legal matters. It is always advisable to consult the necessary authorities, whether or not you choose to represent yourself.

Most countries around the world are dealing with the problem of parental alienation and you can find assistance from the self-help groups within your country.

For a comprehensive discussion of international parental alienation, please refer to:

The International Handbook of Parental Alienation Syndrome, by Richard A Gardner, S. Richard Sauber, Demosthenes Lorandos.

and

Parental Alienation: Science and the Law, by Demosthenes Lorandos and William Bernet.

I know that all of us who are involved in the treatment and legal resolution of parental alienation fervently wish that all alienated parents and children receive justice, and that the repercussions of PA cease to live on in future generations.

We will also continue to strive to address the problems currently faced by alienated parents in the court, Department of Public Social Services, from relevant professionals, and families. It is my hope that we can swiftly move through to the final stage of truth where there is acceptance and the existence and recognition of parental alienation is self-evident.

Appendices

Parental Alienation Laws

BRAZIL

*T*HE PRESIDENT OF THE REPUBLIC let me know that the National Congress decrees and I sanction the following Law:

Art. 1. This Law provides for parental alienation.

Art. 2. An act of parental alienation is considered to be interference in the psychological formation of the child or adolescent promoted or induced by one of the parents, by the grandparents or by those who have the child or adolescent under their authority, custody or surveillance to repudiate the parent or that causes damage to the establishment or maintenance of links with it.

Single paragraph. Exemplary forms of parental alienation, in addition to the acts thus declared by the judge or found by expert examination, performed directly or with the help of third parties:

I - carry out a campaign to disqualify the parent's conduct in the exercise of paternity or maternity;

II - hinder the exercise of parental authority;

III - hinder contact of a child or adolescent with a parent;

IV - hinder the exercise of the regulated right to family life;

V - deliberately omitting relevant personal information about the child or adolescent from the parent, including school, medical and address changes;

VI - to present a false complaint against a parent, against his or her family members or against grandparents, to prevent or hinder their coexistence with the child or adolescent;

VII - change the domicile to a distant place, without justification, aiming at making it difficult for the child or adolescent to live with the other parent, their family members or grandparents.

Art. 3. The practice of parental alienation violates the fundamental right of the child or adolescent to healthy family life, impairs the realization of affection in relationships with the parent and the family group, constitutes moral abuse against the child or adolescent and non-compliance with duties inherent to parental authority or arising from guardianship or custody.

Art. 4. Declared evidence of an act of parental alienation, at request or ex officio, at any procedural moment, in an autonomous or incidental action, the process will have priority processing, and the judge will urgently determine, after hearing the Public Ministry, the provisional measures necessary to preserve the psychological integrity of the child or adolescent, including ensuring their coexistence with the parent or enabling the effective rapprochement between the two, if applicable.

Single paragraph. The child or adolescent and the parent will be guaranteed a minimum guarantee of assisted visitation, except in cases where there is an imminent risk of damage to the physical or psychological integrity of the child or adolescent, attested by a professional eventually appointed by the judge to monitor the visits.

Art. 5. If there is evidence of the practice of parental alienation, in autonomous or incidental action, the judge, if necessary, will determine psychological or biopsychosocial expertise.

1. The expert report will be based on a broad psychological or biopsychosocial assessment, as the case may be, including a personal interview with the parties, examination of documents in the file, history of the couple's relationship and separation, chronology of incidents, personality assessment of those involved and examining how the child or adolescent expresses himself about any accusation against a parent.

2. The expertise will be carried out by a qualified professional or multidisciplinary team, required, in any case, an aptitude proven by professional or academic history to diagnose acts of parental alienation.

3. The expert or multidisciplinary team designated to verify the occurrence of parental alienation shall have a period of 90 (ninety) days to present the report, which can be extended exclusively by judicial authorization based on a detailed justification.

Art. 6. Characterized typical acts of parental alienation or any conduct that makes it difficult for a child or adolescent to live with a parent, in an autonomous or incidental action, the judge may, cumulatively or not, without prejudice to the resulting civil or criminal liability and the wide use of procedural instruments capable of inhibiting or mitigating their effects, depending on the seriousness of the case:

I - declare the occurrence of parental alienation and warn the alienator;

II - expand the family life regime in favor of the alienated parent;

III - stipulate a fine for the alienator;

IV - determine psychological and / or biopsychosocial monitoring;

V - determine the change from custody to shared custody or its inversion;

VI - determine the precautionary fixation of the child's or adolescent's home;

VII - declare the suspension of parental authority.

Single paragraph. Characterized by an abusive change of address, impracticability or obstruction of family life, the judge may also reverse the obligation to take the child or adolescent to or from the parent's residence, during alternating periods of family life.

Art. 7. The allocation or change of custody will be given preference by the parent that enables the effective coexistence of the child or adolescent with the other parent in cases where it is impracticable to custody.

DENMARK

Chapter 1

Introductory provisions

1. Children and young people under 18 are subject to custodial care, unless they are married.
2. *(1)* The holder of custody is obligated to care for the child and can make decisions regarding the child's personal circumstances based on the child's needs and interests.
(2) Children have the right to care and security. Children must be treated with respect for their person and must not

be exposed to corporal punishment or other humiliating treatment.

(3) Parents with custody can dispose of the child's income to a reasonable extent for the child's maintenance and with due consideration for their and the child's position.

3. *(1)* If the parents have joint custody, they must agree on significant decisions regarding the child. The parent with whom the child lives can make decisions about general day-to-day matters relating to the child, including where in Denmark the child will have his or her habitual place of residence.

(2) If the parents have joint custody but disagree about the custody, they both have to give their consent for the child to leave the country, including travels to Greenland or the Faroe Islands. They also have to give their consent if the child's stay abroad, in Greenland or the Faroe Islands is extended beyond the agreed, presumed or specified duration, unless an agreement has been made according to section 17(1), second sentence, or section 25.

4. Decisions made pursuant to the Act will be based on the child's best interests.

5. *(1)* In all matters relating to the child, the child's own views must be taken into consideration, depending on the child's age and maturity.

Chapter 2

Custody holders of custody

6. *(1)* If the parents are married to each other at the time of the child's birth, or if they marry later, they will have joint custody.

(2) If the parents are separated at the time of the child's birth, the mother will, however, have sole custody unless: 1) the separated husband is recognized as the father of the child or his paternity is established by a court judgement or 2) the parents have submitted a declaration according to section 7(1)1; see, however, section 7(2).

(3) If the parents have been married to each other within the ten months immediately preceding the birth of the child, they have joint custody.

7. *(1)* Parents who are not married to each other have joint custody if 1) they, according to the Children Act section 2(1), section 14, subsection (1) or (3), or section 19, cf. section 14, subsection (1) or (3), have submitted a declaration that they will jointly care for and assume responsibility for the child, or 2) they have made an agreement about joint custody according to section 9.

(2) This shall not, however, apply if the declaration in subsection (1)1 has been submitted without the fulfilment of the conditions of section 448(f) of the Danish Administration of Justice Act regarding the processing of cases of custody in Denmark.

(3) If a man is considered to be the father of a child by recognition or because paternity has been established by a court judgment, the parents have joint custody if they have or have had a joint address according to the Danish national register within the ten months immediately preceding the birth of the child.

(4) In cases other than those mentioned in subsections (1)-(3) the mother has sole custody.

8. If the parents share custody, they will continue to have this right even if they have ceased marital relations or have been separated or divorced, or if their marriage has been annulled.

9. Parents can agree to have joint custody. The regional state administration must be notified of the agreement in order for it to be valid. If a custody case has been brought before the court, notification can be made to the court.

10. Parents who have joint custody but do not live together can agree that one of them is to have sole custody. The regional state administration must be notified of the agreement in order for it to be valid. If a custody case has been brought before the court, notification can be made to the court.

11. If non-cohabiting parents with joint custody disagree about custody, the court will decide whether joint custody is to continue or whether one of the parents is to have sole custody. The court can only terminate joint custody for compelling reasons.

12. If an agreement is made under section 10 or a decision is made under section 11 granting sole custody to one of the parents, joint custody will be reinstated if married parents, including separated parents, resume or continue marital relations.

Transfer of custody

13. *(1)* Parents can agree to transfer custody from one parent to the other. The regional state administration must be notified of the agreement in order for it to be valid. If a custody case has been brought before the court, notification can be made to the court.

(2) Custody can be transferred to an individual or individuals other than the parents, by an agreement approved by the

regional state administration. Custody can be transferred to a married couple jointly, including the other parent and his/her spouse. If a custody case has been brought before the court, the court can approve the agreement.

14. *(1)* On the request of a parent who does not have custody, the court can order joint custody or transfer custody to this parent.

(2) The court can change an agreement under section 13(2) or can change a decision under section 15.

Death

15. *(1)* If the parents have joint custody and one of them dies, the surviving parent will continue to have custody. If, at the time of the death, the child's place of residence was not with the surviving parent, another person can apply to be awarded custody in connection with the death. The application can only be granted if it is not considered in the child's best interests for the surviving parent to continue to have custody. If the child's place of residence was with the surviving parent at the time of the death, and if the surviving parent caused the death of the other holder of custody, another person can apply to be awarded custody. The application can only be granted if it is crucial to the child's best interests that the surviving parent does not continue to have custody.

(2) In the event of the death of a parent with sole custody, or in any other circumstance in which a death means that the child has no person with custody for it, a decision will be made as to who should have custody, based on the child's best interests. If the surviving parent applies for custody,

the application will be granted unless it is not considered to be in the child's best interests.

(3) In the event that a parent with sole custody caused the death of the other parent, another person can apply to be awarded custody. The application can only be granted if it is crucial to the child's best interests that the surviving parent does not continue to have custody.

(4) Custody can be awarded to a married couple jointly, including the surviving parent and his/her spouse.

16. The holders of custody can appoint an individual or individuals to whom custody should be awarded after their death. The preferential status of the surviving parent according to section 15 will apply regardless of whether other persons are named.

Chapter 3

Child's place of residence and advance notice of impending move

17. *(1)* If the parents have joint custody and disagree about which parent the child should live with, the court will decide the matter. The court can decide that the child can live with a parent who lives, or wants to live, abroad or in Greenland or the Faroe Islands.

(2) The court can change an agreement or a decision about a child's place of residence.

18. A parent intending to change his or her place of residence or that of the child to another location in Denmark or abroad is required to inform the other parent of this intention not later than six weeks before the impending move.

Chapter 4

Contact, etc. Contact with parents

19. *(1)* Attempts should be made to maintain the child's connection with both parents by ensuring that the child has contact with the parent with whom the child does not live (the non- resident parent). Both parents are responsible for ensuring that the child has contact.

(2) The parent with whom the child does not live can apply for contact rights.

(3) If there is no or only an extremely limited amount of contact, the parent with whom the child lives can ask the regional state administration to summon the other parent for a meeting about contact.

Contact with persons other than the parents

20. *(1)* If one or both parents are dead, contact rights can be granted to the nearest relatives to whom child is closely attached.

(2) If the child does not have contact with the non-resident parent or has only extremely limited contact with this parent, in exceptional circumstances contact rights can be granted to the nearest relatives to whom the child is closely attached.

(3) The child's closest relatives can apply for contact rights.

Decisions regarding contact

21. *(1)* If the parents disagree about the extent of contact and contact arrangements, they can ask for a decision to be made about the matter and for the necessary conditions regarding contact to be specified.

(2) Contact can be specified for up to 7 out of 14 days.

(3) The regional state administration can make a decision about the child's transport in connection with contact and about the payment of the related costs.

(4) The regional state administration can refuse to grant contact rights and can change or revoke a decision about contact.

Other forms of contact

22. *(1)* In special cases, a decision may be made about other forms of contact with the child such as phone calls, letters, e-mails, photographs, and similar.

(2) A request for other forms of contact may be made by: 1) the parent with whom the child does not live, or 2) the child's closest relatives, provided the conditions for granting contact rights set out in section 20 have been met. *(3)* Section 21, subsections (1) and (4) may be similarly applied.

Information about the child

23. *(1)* The parent who does not have custody has the right to request information about the child from schools, daycare facilities, the social and healthcare system, private hospitals, and private GPs and dentists. This parent also has the right to receive documents about the child if such information is available at the schools and daycare institutions. Confidential information about the holder of custody may not be passed on.

(2) The parent who does not have custody has the right to request and receive information about general social activities at the child's school or daycare institution from the school or institution in question, and is entitled to participate in these activities.

(3) The institutions, etc., mentioned in subsections (1) and (2) can refuse to give specific information or hand out documents relating to the child. They can refuse to provide information about activities and deny admission to the activities, if they consider giving the parent admission to such activities would be damaging to the child.

(4) In special cases, at the request of the holder of custody or one of the institutions mentioned in subsections (1) and (2), the regional state administration can withdraw the right of the parent who does not have custody to receive information and documents in accordance with subsection (1), or to receive information about activities and to take part in them pursuant to subsection (2). The decision will take effect from the date on which the institution, etc., is notified of the decision.

Contact with children in care

24. The provisions governing contact and other forms of contact contained in this Act cannot be applied if a child has been put into care outside the home in accordance with Chapter 11 of the Consolidation Act on Social Services.

Decisions about foreign travel

25. Even if parents with joint custody disagree about custody, the regional state administration can decide that one of the parents can take the child abroad or to Greenland or the Faroe Islands for a short period.

Chapter 5

Temporary decisions

Custody and the child's place of residence

26. *(1)* During a custody case, the authority handling the case can, on request, decide who should have temporary custody or which parent the child should live with temporarily. During a case about the child's place of residence, on request, the authority can decide which parent the child should live with temporarily.

(2) A decision pursuant to subsection (1) will apply until a final enforceable agreement or decision has been made.

(3) A decision made by the regional state administration under subsection (1) will lapse: 1) four weeks after it has notified the parties of the conclusion of the case, cf. section 40, unless one of the parties has applied within this time limit for the case to be brought before the court, 2) if the case is withdrawn or dismissed after being brought to court, or 3) if marital relations are resumed.

27. If the parents have joint custody and a risk exists that one of them will take the child out of the country and thus pre-empt a decision about custody, the Minister for Family and Consumer Affairs, or a person authorized by the minister, can temporarily grant sole custody to the other parent.

28. If the holder or both holders of custody are prevented from making decisions about the child's personal circumstances, the regional state administration will decide where to place custody during the period in which the parents are prevented from making decisions.

Contact, etc.

29. During a case about custody, the child's place of residence, contact or other form of contact, on request, the regional state administration can make a decision about temporary contact or other form of contact. If a custody case has been brought before the court under section 40, and if the court case concerns contact or other form of contact under section 38(2), on request, the court can make a decision about temporary contact or other form of contact.

(2) A decision pursuant to subsection (1) will apply until a final enforceable decision about contact, a temporary decision about contact or an agreement about another form of contact has been made.

(3) In highly exceptional circumstances, the powers conferred by subsection (1) to make a temporary decision can also be exercised by the Minister for Family and Consumer Affairs.

Changes

30. A temporary decision made under sections 26-29 can be changed.

Chapter 6

Case processing initiation

31. *(1)* An application for a decision about custody under sections 11, 14 or 15, about the child's place of residence under section 17, and about contact, etc., under sections

19-22 and section 25 must be submitted to the regional state administration.

(2) The regional state administration will call the parties to a meeting unless the application relates exclusively to a decision regarding other forms of contact under section 22.

(3) The regional state administration need not call the parties to a meeting if it is considered unnecessary or inappropriate.

Child welfare counselling and family mediation

32. *(1)* The regional state administration must offer parents and children child welfare counselling or family mediation in cases of disagreement about custody, the child's place of residence or contact.

(2) In other circumstances, the regional state administration can offer child welfare counselling or family mediation if there is a special need.

(3) The regional state administration need not offer child welfare counselling or family mediation under subsection (1) if it is considered unnecessary or inappropriate.

Child welfare consultations

33. *(1)* The regional state administration can initiate child welfare consultations in cases about custody, the child's place of residence and contact.

(2) If the regional state administration has initiated a child welfare consultation, this must be completed before the case can be brought before the court under section 40.

The child's perspective

34. *(1)* The child's views must be taken into consideration during a case about custody, the child's place of residence or contact by giving the child the opportunity to make its views and opinions known. Information about the child's perspective can be gained through personal interviews, statements from child welfare consultants or other ways that shed light on the child's point of view.
(2) The obligation to directly take the child's views into consideration in the case does not apply if this is deemed to be damaging to him or her or considered unnecessary given the circumstances of the case.

The child's right to contact the regional state administration

35. A child who has reached the age of 10 can ask the regional state administration to call the parents to a meeting about custody, the child's place of residence or contact.

Declaration from the parents in certain cases

36. *(1)* Before approving a custody agreement under section 13(2) or making a decision about custody under section 15(2), the regional state administration must obtain a declaration from the parent who does not have custody.
(2) Before making a decision about contact under section 20(2), the regional state administration must obtain a declaration from the parent who does not have contact or has only extremely limited contact.

(3) A declaration need not be obtained under subsection (1) or (2) if this is considered to be damaging to the child or would disproportionately delay the case.

Custody after death

37. Under section 15, the regional state administration makes decisions about custody in the event of death. The regional state administration will bring the case before the court if so requested by a party within four weeks of the party's being informed about the decision.

Decisions about contact, etc.

38. *(1)* The regional state administration makes decisions about contact and other forms of contact subject to sections 19-22 and section 25.

(2) If a case about custody under section 11 or about the child's place of residence under section 17 is brought to court under section 40, each parent may apply for a decision also to be made during the court proceedings about issues regarding contact and other forms of contact under section 21, cf. section 19, and sections 22 and 25. The same applies during a case under section 14(1), when an unmarried father has not had custody and the case is brought before the court for the first time.

39. An application for a change in contact or other forms of contact can be refused if there has been no significant change in circumstances.

Concluding the processing of a case and bringing it before the court

40. *(1)* The regional state administration can conclude a case about custody under section 11 or section 14 or about the child's place of residence under section 17 if agreement has not been reached regarding custody or place of residence. The regional state administration will bring the case before the court if so requested by a party within four weeks of the party's being informed about the conclusion of the case. This does not apply if the case has been concluded because the party in question failed to attend a meeting at the regional state administration.

(2) On the application of one of the parties, the regional state administration can conclude a case and bring it before the court if: 1) the parties have been counselled at a meeting at the regional state administration without reaching agreement about custody or the child's place of residence, and the parties or one of the parties does not want child welfare counselling or family mediation, or if child welfare counselling or family mediation has ended without agreement being reached, or 2) the party in question has attended a meeting whereas the other party has failed to appear despite being called in twice.

(3) In special circumstances, on application, the regional state administration can conclude the case and bring it before the court although the conditions of subsection (1) or (2) have not been met.

Appeals, etc.

41. *(1)* In accordance with the provisions of this Act, decisions made by the regional state administration can be appealed to the Minister for Family and Consumer Affairs, cf. however, subsections (2) and (3).

(2) Appeals may not be lodged against decisions made under section 37 and section 40, subsections (1) and (2), decisions granting applications under section 40(3), and decisions refusing applications under section 46(2), cf. subsection (1).

(3) Decisions made according to section 23(3) can be appealed to the regional state administration. This does not apply to decisions made by the healthcare system, however. A decision made by the regional state administration cannot be brought before a higher administrative authority. On application, however, the Minister for Family and Consumer Affairs can decide to process a case if the case is deemed to be fundamentally or significantly important.

Powers

42. The Minister for Family and Consumer Affairs can lay down rules: 1) for the processing of cases about custody, the child's place of residence, contact, etc., 2) for the processing of cases regarding the transport of the child in connection with contact, including the parents' payment of the related costs, 3) about supervised contact, 4) about the notification of custody agreements, 5) about child welfare counselling, child welfare consultations and family mediation and 6) about the processing of appeals.

Chapter 7

Work agreements

43. If a child or young person under custody, cf. section 1, with the permission of the holder of custody, has independently undertaken to perform a service or other personal work enabling him to maintain himself, the young person in question, if aged 15 or over, can personally terminate the agreement and undertake work of a similar nature, unless the holder of custody decides otherwise.

44. The holder of custody can terminate an agreement to perform a service or other personal work entered into by the young person if necessary in the interests of the upbringing or welfare of the child or young person. However, as far as possible, the agreement should be terminated with an appropriate period of notice and, where reasonable, compensation should be made to the other party.

Chapter 8

International agreements and international jurisdiction

45. *(1)* The government can sign agreements with other states concerning the relationship between the rules of Danish law and the rules of foreign law governing custody, place of residence, contact and other forms of contact. Such agreements will apply in Denmark following the publication of a notice in the Danish Law Gazette ("Lovtidende").

(2) The Minister for Family and Consumer Affairs can furthermore lay down rules for the relationship between

Denmark's rules and the rules of other Nordic countries regarding custody, the child's place of residence, contact and other forms of contact.

(3) The Minister for Family and Consumer Affairs can lay down rules for the processing of cases in pursuance of this Act, which is comprised by the Hague Convention of 19 October 1996 on Jurisdiction, Applicable Law, Recognition, Enforcement and Co-operation in Respect of Parental Responsibility and Measures for the Protection of Children (the Hague convention for the protection of children).

46. *(1)* The regional state administration can process a case regarding custody, the child's place of residence, contact, etc., providing the conditions of section 448(f) of the Danish Administration of Justice Act have been met.

(2) A refusal by the regional state administration to process a case regarding custody and the child's place of residence according to sections 11, 14, 15 and 17 that does not meet the conditions contained in subsection (1) can be brought before the court, on the application of one of the parties.

Chapter 9

Commencement, etc.

47. *(1)* This Act comes into force on 1 October 2007.
(2) The Danish act on custody and access, cf. the consolidation act no. 39 of 15 January 2007, will be abolished.
48. Section 6(2)1, section 6(3) and section 7(3) apply only to children born on 1 October 2007 or later.
49. This Act will not apply to the Faroe Islands and Greenland but may, by Royal Decree, become effective

for the Faroe Islands and Greenland with such changes as follow from the special circumstances in the Faroe Islands and Greenland.

MEXICO

In 2004, the Federal District of Mexico was the first jurisdiction to adopt a reference to PA in its civil code:

Article 411: Whoever exercises parental authority must ensure respect and consistent contact of the children with the other parent who also exercises custody. Accordingly, each parent must avoid any act of manipulation, parental alienation aimed at producing in the child resentment or rejection of the other parent.

In 2006, however, lobbying spearheaded by some special interest groups, which included *ad hominem* attacks on Richard Gardner, led to the elimination of the reference. The same article was later adopted into the civil code of the state of Morelos, Mexico, as Article 224. Further, in 2007, the state of Aguascalientes, Mexico, modified the civil code by addition of language that prohibited parents from engaging in PA, empowered courts, and mandated that the courts order "therapeutic measures necessary . . . in order to restore healthy contact with both parents." In doing so, the law in Agusascalientes authorized "enforcement measures" to be used by courts including but not limited to "suspension of . . . custody or contact" if necessary.

In June 2011, the state of Queretaro, Mexico, approved the inclusion of PA in its civil code, Articles 443 to 449, acknowledging that the behavior is "a form of abuse of minors." After revision, the Civil Code Article 443 allows parental authority to be suspended for "engaging in behaviors of parental alienation." Similar parliamentary proposals for including definitions of PA in the Civil Code have been made in Mexican states of Michoacan de Ocampo, Chihuahua, and Morelos.

On May 16, 2018, the Supreme Court of Mexico ruled on the constitutionality of the articles 336 Bis B, 429 Bis A and 459, fraction IV, and Decree 1380 of the Civil Code for the State of Oaxaca, which outlawed PA. The Court found the language of the original Act to be too punitive toward alienating parents because the Act violated "the principle of proportionality" by threatening to revoke parental authority entirely in cases of PA. The original statute did not give judges the ability to weigh the "best interest" of the child when considering the remedy to PA. Nevertheless, the Supreme Court upheld the concept of PA and ruled in favor of editing the legislation.

CALIFORNIA

01/03/18 07:36 PM
RN 18 00287 PAGE 1

67082

LEGISLATIVE COUNSEL'S DIGEST

Bill No.
as introduced, _____.
General Subject: Professional training: coursework: parental alienation.

Existing law requires persons applying for initial licensure or renewal of a license as a psychologist, clinical social worker, professional clinical counselor, or marriage and family therapist to have completed prescribed coursework or training in child abuse assessment and reporting, as established by the Board of Psychology and the Board of Behavioral Sciences. Existing law requires the initial training to include, among other components, a minimum of 7 contact hours, various indicators of abuse, crisis counseling techniques, and community resources. Existing law also requires that a licensed psychologist, a licensed educational psychologist, clinical social worker, professional clinical counselor, and marriage and family therapist certify that he or she has completed not less than 36 hours of approved continuing education to renew his or her license.

This bill would also require that both the initial training and the continuing education described above for these professionals include the study of parental alienation and its diagnostic indicators. By expanding the scope of the crime of perjury, the bill would impose a state-mandated local program.

The California Constitution requires the state to reimburse local agencies and school districts for certain costs mandated by the state. Statutory provisions establish procedures for making that reimbursement.

This bill would provide that no reimbursement is required by this act for a specified reason.

Vote: majority. Appropriation: no. Fiscal committee: yes. State-mandated local program: yes.

01/03/18 07:36 PM
67082   RN 18 00287 PAGE 2

THE PEOPLE OF THE STATE OF CALIFORNIA DO ENACT AS FOLLOWS:

SECTION 1. Section 28 of the Business and Professions Code is amended to read:

28. (a) The Legislature finds that there is a need to ensure that professionals of the healing arts who have demonstrable contact with victims and potential victims of child, elder, and dependent adult abuse, and abusers and potential abusers of children, elders, and dependent adults are provided with adequate and appropriate training regarding the assessment and reporting of child, elder, and dependent adult abuse that will ameliorate, reduce, and eliminate the trauma of abuse and neglect and ensure the reporting of abuse in a timely manner to prevent additional occurrences.

(b) The Board of Psychology and the Board of Behavioral Sciences shall establish required training in the area of child abuse assessment and reporting for all persons applying for initial licensure and renewal of a license as a psychologist, clinical social worker, professional clinical counselor, or marriage and family therapist. This training shall be required one time only for all persons applying for initial licensure or for licensure renewal.

(c) All persons applying for initial licensure or renewal of a license as a psychologist, clinical social worker, professional clinical counselor, or marriage and family therapist shall, in addition to all other requirements for licensure or renewal, have completed coursework or training in child abuse assessment and reporting that meets the requirements of this section, including detailed knowledge of the Child Abuse and Neglect Reporting Act (Article 2.5 (commencing with Section 11164) of Chapter 2 of Title 1 of Part 4 of the Penal Code). The training shall meet all of the following requirements:

(1) Be obtained from one of the following sources:

(A) An accredited or approved educational institution, as defined in Sections 2902, 4980.36, 4980.37, 4996.18, and 4999.12, including extension courses offered by those institutions.

(B) A continuing education provider as specified by the responsible board by regulation.

(C) A course sponsored or offered by a professional association or a local, county, or state department of health or mental health for continuing education and approved or accepted by the responsible board.

(2) Have a minimum of seven contact hours.

(3) Include the study of the assessment and method of reporting of sexual assault, neglect, severe neglect, general neglect, willful cruelty or unjustifiable punishment, corporal punishment or injury, and abuse in out-of-home care. The training shall also include physical and behavioral indicators of abuse, crisis counseling techniques, community resources, rights and responsibilities of reporting, consequences of failure to report, caring for a child's needs after a report is made, sensitivity to previously abused children and adults, and implications and methods of treatment for children and adults. adults, and parental alienation and its diagnostic indicators.

(4) An applicant shall provide the appropriate board with documentation of completion of the required child abuse training.

(d) The Board of Psychology and the Board of Behavioral Sciences shall exempt an applicant who applies for an exemption from this section and who shows to the

193

satisfaction of the board that there would be no need for the training in his or her practice because of the nature of that practice.

(e) It is the intent of the Legislature that a person licensed as a psychologist, clinical social worker, professional clinical counselor, or marriage and family therapist have minimal but appropriate training in the areas of child, elder, and dependent adult abuse assessment and reporting. It is not intended that, by solely complying with this section, a practitioner is fully trained in the subject of treatment of child, elder, and dependent adult abuse victims and abusers.

(f) The Board of Psychology and the Board of Behavioral Sciences are encouraged to include coursework regarding the assessment and reporting of elder and dependent adult abuse in the required training on aging and long-term care issues prior to licensure or license renewal.

SEC. 2. Section 2915 of the Business and Professions Code is amended to read:

2915. (a) Except as provided in this section, the board shall issue a renewal license only to an applicant who has completed 36 hours of approved continuing professional development in the preceding two years.

(b) Each person who applies to renew or reinstate his or her license issued pursuant to this chapter shall certify under penalty of perjury that he or she is in compliance with this section and shall retain proof of this compliance for submission to the board upon request. False statements submitted pursuant to this section shall be a violation of Section 2970.

(c) Continuing professional development means certain continuing education learning activities approved in four different categories:

(1) Professional.

(2) Academic.

(3) Sponsored continuing education ~~coursework.~~ coursework, which shall include training in parental alienation and its diagnostic indicators.

(4) Board certification from the American Board of Professional Psychology.

The board may develop regulations further defining acceptable continuing professional development activities.

(d) (1) The board shall require a licensed psychologist who began graduate study prior to January 1, 2004, to take a continuing education course during his or her first renewal period after the operative date of this section in spousal or partner abuse assessment, detection, and intervention strategies, including community resources, cultural factors, and same gender abuse dynamics. Equivalent courses in spousal or partner abuse assessment, detection, and intervention strategies taken prior to the operative date of this section or proof of equivalent teaching or practice experience may be submitted to the board and at its discretion, may be accepted in satisfaction of this requirement.

(2) Continuing education courses taken pursuant to this subdivision shall be applied to the 36 hours of approved continuing professional development required under subdivision (a).

(e) Continuing education courses approved to meet the requirements of this section shall be approved by organizations approved by the board. An organization previously approved by the board to provide or approve continuing education is deemed approved under this section.

01/03/18 07:36 PM
67082   RN 18 00287 PAGE 4

(f) The board may accept continuing education courses approved by an entity that has demonstrated to the board in writing that it has, at a minimum, a 10-year history of providing educational programming for psychologists and has documented procedures for maintaining a continuing education approval program. The board shall adopt regulations necessary for implementing this section.

(g) The board may grant an exemption, or an extension of the time for compliance with, from the continuing professional development requirement of this section.

(h) The administration of this section may be funded through professional license fees and continuing education provider and course approval fees, or both. The fees related to the administration of this section shall not exceed the costs of administering the corresponding provisions of this section.

SEC. 3.   Section 4980.54 of the Business and Professions Code is amended to read:

4980.54.   (a) The Legislature recognizes that the education and experience requirements in this chapter constitute only minimal requirements to ensure that an applicant is prepared and qualified to take the licensure examinations as specified in subdivision (d) of Section 4980.40 and, if he or she passes those examinations, to begin practice.

(b) In order to continuously improve the competence of licensed marriage and family therapists and as a model for all psychotherapeutic professions, the Legislature encourages all licensees to regularly engage in continuing education related to the profession or scope of practice as defined in this chapter.

(c) Except as provided in subdivision (e), the board shall not renew any license pursuant to this chapter unless the applicant certifies to the board, on a form prescribed by the board, that he or she has completed not less than 36 hours of approved continuing education in or relevant to the field of marriage and family therapy in the preceding two years, as determined by the board.

(d) The board shall have the right to audit the records of any applicant to verify the completion of the continuing education requirement. Applicants shall maintain records of completion of required continuing education coursework for a minimum of two years and shall make these records available to the board for auditing purposes upon request.

(e) The board may establish exceptions from the continuing education requirements of this section for good cause, as defined by the board.

(f) The continuing education shall be obtained from one of the following sources:

(1) An accredited school or state-approved school that meets the requirements set forth in Section 4980.36 or 4980.37. Nothing in this paragraph shall be construed as requiring coursework to be offered as part of a regular degree program.

(2) Other continuing education providers, as specified by the board by regulation.

(g) The board shall establish, by regulation, a procedure for identifying acceptable providers of continuing education courses, and all providers of continuing education, as described in paragraphs (1) and (2) of subdivision (f), shall adhere to procedures established by the board. The board may revoke or deny the right of a provider to offer continuing education coursework pursuant to this section for failure to comply with this section or any regulation adopted pursuant to this section.

(h) Training, education, and coursework by approved providers shall incorporate one or more of the following:

01/03/18 07:36 PM
67082   RN 18 00287 PAGE 5

(1) Aspects of the discipline that are fundamental to the understanding or the practice of marriage and family therapy.

(2) Aspects of the discipline of marriage and family therapy in which significant recent developments have occurred.

(3) Aspects of other disciplines that enhance the understanding or the practice of marriage and family therapy.

(i) A system of continuing education for licensed marriage and family therapists shall include courses directly related to the diagnosis, assessment, and treatment of the client population being ~~served.~~ served, and shall include training in parental alienation and its diagnostic indicators.

(j) The board shall, by regulation, fund the administration of this section through continuing education provider fees to be deposited in the Behavioral Sciences Fund. The fees related to the administration of this section shall be sufficient to meet, but shall not exceed, the costs of administering the corresponding provisions of this section. For purposes of this subdivision, a provider of continuing education as described in paragraph (1) of subdivision (f) shall be deemed to be an approved provider.

(k) The continuing education requirements of this section shall comply fully with the guidelines for mandatory continuing education established by the Department of Consumer Affairs pursuant to Section 166.

SEC. 4. Section 4989.34 of the Business and Professions Code is amended to read:

4989.34. (a) To renew his or her license, a licensee shall certify to the board, on a form prescribed by the board, completion in the preceding two years of not less than 36 hours of approved continuing education in, or relevant to, educational psychology.

(b) (1) The continuing education shall be obtained from either an accredited university or a continuing education provider as specified by the board by regulation.

(2) The board shall establish, by regulation, a procedure identifying acceptable providers of continuing education courses, and all providers of continuing education shall comply with procedures established by the board. The board may revoke or deny the right of a provider to offer continuing education coursework pursuant to this section for failure to comply with this section or any regulation adopted pursuant to this section.

(c) (1) Training, education, and coursework by approved providers shall incorporate one or more of the following:

~~(1)~~

(A) Aspects of the discipline that are fundamental to the understanding or the practice of educational psychology.

~~(2)~~

(B) Aspects of the discipline of educational psychology in which significant recent developments have occurred.

~~(3)~~

(C) Aspects of other disciplines that enhance the understanding or the practice of educational psychology.

(2) Continuing education for licensed educational psychologists shall also include training in parental alienation and its diagnostic indicators.

(d) The board may audit the records of a licensee to verify completion of the continuing education requirement. A licensee shall maintain records of the completion

01/03/18 07:36 PM
67082   RN 18 00287 PAGE 6

of required continuing education coursework for a minimum of two years and shall make these records available to the board for auditing purposes upon its request.

(e) The board may establish exceptions from the continuing education requirements of this section for good cause, as determined by the board.

(f) The board shall, by regulation, fund the administration of this section through continuing education provider fees to be deposited in the Behavioral Sciences Fund. The amount of the fees shall be sufficient to meet, but shall not exceed, the costs of administering this section.

(g) The continuing education requirements of this section shall comply fully with the guidelines for mandatory continuing education established by the Department of Consumer Affairs pursuant to Section 166.

SEC. 5. Section 4996.2 of the Business and Professions Code is amended to read:

4996.2. Each applicant for a license shall furnish evidence satisfactory to the board that he or she complies with all of the following requirements:

(a) Is at least 21 years of age.

(b) Has received a master's degree from an accredited school of social work.

(c) Has had two years of supervised post-master's degree experience, as specified in Section 4996.23.

(d) Has not committed any crimes or acts constituting grounds for denial of licensure under Section 480. The board shall not issue a registration or license to any person who has been convicted of any crime in this or another state or in a territory of the United States that involves sexual abuse of children or who is required to register pursuant to Section 290 of the Penal Code or the equivalent in another state or territory.

(e) Has completed adequate instruction and training in the subject of alcoholism and other chemical substance dependency. This requirement applies only to applicants who matriculate on or after January 1, 1986.

(f) Has completed instruction and training in spousal or partner abuse assessment, detection, and intervention. This requirement applies to an applicant who began graduate training during the period commencing on January 1, 1995, and ending on December 31, 2003. An applicant who began graduate training on or after January 1, 2004, shall complete a minimum of 15 contact hours of coursework in spousal or partner abuse assessment, detection, and intervention strategies, including knowledge of community resources, cultural factors, and same gender abuse dynamics. Coursework required under this subdivision may be satisfactory if taken either in fulfillment of other educational requirements for licensure or in a separate course.

(g) Has completed a minimum of 10 contact hours of training or coursework in human sexuality as specified in Section 1807 of Title 16 of the California Code of Regulations. This training or coursework may be satisfactory if taken either in fulfillment of other educational requirements for licensure or in a separate course.

(h) Has completed a minimum of seven contact hours of training or coursework in child abuse assessment and reporting as specified in ~~Section 1807.2 of Title 16 of the California Code of Regulations.~~ paragraph (3) of subdivision (c) of Section 28, and any regulations promulgated under that section. This training or coursework may be satisfactory if taken either in fulfillment of other educational requirements for licensure or in a separate course.

You're not Crazy

SEC. 6.   Section 4996.22 of the Business and Professions Code is amended to read:

4996.22. (a) (1) Except as provided in subdivision (c), the board shall not renew any license pursuant to this chapter unless the applicant certifies to the board, on a form prescribed by the board, that he or she has completed not less than 36 hours of approved continuing education in or relevant to the field of social work in the preceding two years, as determined by the board.

(2) The board shall not renew any license of an applicant who began graduate study prior to January 1, 2004, pursuant to this chapter unless the applicant certifies to the board that during the applicant's first renewal period after the operative date of this section, he or she completed a continuing education course in spousal or partner abuse assessment, detection, and intervention strategies, including community resources, cultural factors, and same gender abuse dynamics. On and after January 1, 2005, the course shall consist of not less than seven hours of training. Equivalent courses in spousal or partner abuse assessment, detection, and intervention strategies taken prior to the operative date of this section or proof of equivalent teaching or practice experience may be submitted to the board and at its discretion, may be accepted in satisfaction of this requirement. Continuing education courses taken pursuant to this paragraph shall be applied to the 36 hours of approved continuing education required under paragraph (1).

(b) The board shall have the right to audit the records of any applicant to verify the completion of the continuing education requirement. Applicants shall maintain records of completion of required continuing education coursework for a minimum of two years and shall make these records available to the board for auditing purposes upon request.

(c) The board may establish exceptions from the continuing education requirement of this section for good cause as defined by the board.

(d) The continuing education shall be obtained from one of the following sources:

(1) An accredited school of social work, as defined in Section 4991.2, or a school or department of social work that is a candidate for accreditation by the Commission on Accreditation of the Council on Social Work Education. Nothing in this paragraph shall be construed as requiring coursework to be offered as part of a regular degree program.

(2) Other continuing education providers, as specified by the board by regulation.

(e) The board shall establish, by regulation, a procedure for identifying acceptable providers of continuing education courses, and all providers of continuing education, as described in paragraphs (1) and (2) of subdivision (d), shall adhere to the procedures established by the board. The board may revoke or deny the right of a provider to offer continuing education coursework pursuant to this section for failure to comply with this section or any regulation adopted pursuant to this section.

(f) Training, education, and coursework by approved providers shall incorporate one or more of the following:

(1) Aspects of the discipline that are fundamental to the understanding, or the practice, of social work.

(2) Aspects of the social work discipline in which significant recent developments have occurred.

198

01/03/18 07:36 PM
67082   RN 18 00287 PAGE 8

(3) Aspects of other related disciplines that enhance the understanding, or the practice, of social work.

(g) A system of continuing education for licensed clinical social workers shall include courses directly related to the diagnosis, assessment, and treatment of the client population being ~~served.~~ served, and shall also include training in parental alienation and its diagnostic indicators.

(h) The continuing education requirements of this section shall comply fully with the guidelines for mandatory continuing education established by the Department of Consumer Affairs pursuant to Section 166.

(i) The board may adopt regulations as necessary to implement this section.

(j) The board shall, by regulation, fund the administration of this section through continuing education provider fees to be deposited in the Behavioral Sciences Fund. The fees related to the administration of this section shall be sufficient to meet, but shall not exceed, the costs of administering the corresponding provisions of this section. For purposes of this subdivision, a provider of continuing education as described in paragraph (1) of subdivision (d) shall be deemed to be an approved provider.

SEC. 7.   Section 4999.76 of the Business and Professions Code is amended to read:

4999.76.   (a) Except as provided in subdivision (c), the board shall not renew any license pursuant to this chapter unless the applicant certifies to the board, on a form prescribed by the board, that he or she has completed not less than 36 hours of approved continuing education in or relevant to the field of professional clinical counseling in the preceding two years, as determined by the board.

(b) The board shall have the right to audit the records of any applicant to verify the completion of the continuing education requirement. Applicants shall maintain records of completed continuing education coursework for a minimum of two years and shall make these records available to the board for auditing purposes upon request.

(c) The board may establish exceptions from the continuing education requirement of this section for good cause, as defined by the board.

(d) The continuing education shall be obtained from one of the following sources:

(1) A school, college, or university that is accredited or approved, as defined in Section 4999.12. Nothing in this paragraph shall be construed as requiring coursework to be offered as part of a regular degree program.

(2) Other continuing education providers as specified by the board by regulation.

(e) The board shall establish, by regulation, a procedure for identifying acceptable providers of continuing education courses, and all providers of continuing education, as described in paragraphs (1) and (2) of subdivision (d), shall adhere to procedures established by the board. The board may revoke or deny the right of a provider to offer continuing education coursework pursuant to this section for failure to comply with this section or any regulation adopted pursuant to this section.

(f) Training, education, and coursework by approved providers shall incorporate one or more of the following:

(1) Aspects of the discipline that are fundamental to the understanding or the practice of professional clinical counseling.

(2) Significant recent developments in the discipline of professional clinical counseling.

01/03/18 07:36 PM
RN 18 00287 PAGE 9
67082

(3) Aspects of other disciplines that enhance the understanding or the practice of professional clinical counseling.

(g) A system of continuing education for licensed professional clinical counselors shall include courses directly related to the diagnosis, assessment, and treatment of the client population being ~~served.~~ served, and shall also include training in parental alienation and its diagnostic indicators.

(h) The board shall, by regulation, fund the administration of this section through continuing education provider fees to be deposited in the Behavioral Sciences Fund. The fees related to the administration of this section shall be sufficient to meet, but shall not exceed, the costs of administering the corresponding provisions of this section. For the purposes of this subdivision, a provider of continuing education as described in paragraph (1) of subdivision (d) shall be deemed to be an approved provider.

(i) The continuing education requirements of this section shall fully comply with the guidelines for mandatory continuing education established by the Department of Consumer Affairs pursuant to Section 166.

SEC. 8. No reimbursement is required by this act pursuant to Section 6 of Article XIII B of the California Constitution because the only costs that may be incurred by a local agency or school district will be incurred because this act creates a new crime or infraction, eliminates a crime or infraction, or changes the penalty for a crime or infraction, within the meaning of Section 17556 of the Government Code, or changes the definition of a crime within the meaning of Section 6 of Article XIII B of the California Constitution.

- 0 -

FLORIDA

Below is a similar bill in the State of Florida. (Suz Remus is the person to contact there if you can help. She has worked tirelessly to get this passed).

- 1 A bill to be entitled
- 2 An act relating to child psychological abuse; amending
- 3 s. 39.01, F.S.; revising the definition of the term
- 4 "harm"; amending s. 39.201, F.S.; revising a provision
- 5 relating to mandatory reporting requirements for child
- 6 abuse, abandonment, or neglect to include child
- 7 psychological abuse; requiring the Board of Psychology
- 8 within the Department of Health to revise the
- 9 continuing education requirements for renewal of a
- 10 license to practice psychology to include child
- 11 psychological abuse; providing an effective date.
- 12 13 Be It Enacted by the Legislature of the State of Florida: 14
- 15 Section 1. Paragraph (m) is added to subsection (30) of
- 16 section 39.01, Florida Statutes, to read:
- 17 39.01 Definitions.—When used in this chapter, unless the
- 18 context otherwise requires:

- 19 (30) "Harm" to a child's health or welfare can occur when
- 20 any person:
- 21 (m) Inflicts mental injury, as defined in subsection (42),
- 22 on a child through the use of manipulation or psychological
- 23 abuse, including, but not limited to, parental alienation, which
- 24 creates a significant developmental pathology, personality
- 25 disorder pathology, or delusional-psychiatric pathology as
- Page1 of 2 CODING: Words stricken are deletions; words underlined are additions.

HB 1279-00

FLORIDA HOUSE OF REPRESENTATIVES

- 26 diagnosed by a mental health professional licensed under chapter
- 27 490 or chapter 491.
- 28 Section 2. Paragraph (a) of subsection (1) of section
- 29 39.201, Florida Statutes, is amended to read:
- 30 39.201 Mandatory reports of child abuse, abandonment, or
- 31 neglect; mandatory reports of death; central abuse hotline.—
- 32 (1)(a) Any person who knows, or has reasonable cause to

- 33 suspect, that a child is abused, abandoned, or neglected by a
- 34 parent, legal custodian, caregiver, or other person responsible
- 35 for the child's welfare, as defined in this chapter, or that a
- 36 child is in need of supervision and care and has no parent,
- 37 legal custodian, or responsible adult relative immediately known
- 38 and available to provide supervision and care shall report such
- 39 knowledge or suspicion to the department in the manner
- 40 prescribed in subsection (2). For purposes of the mandatory
- 41 reporting requirements in this section, child abuse includes any
- 42 harm or mental injury as those terms are defined in s. 39.01.
- 43 Section 3. The Board of Psychology within the Department
- 44 of Health shall revise the requirements for renewal of a license
- 45 to practice psychology, pursuant to s. 490.007, Florida
- 46 Statutes, to require continuing education regarding child
- 47 psychological abuse, including, but not limited to, abuse

- 48 through the use of manipulation or parental alienation.
- 49 Section 4. This act shall take effect July 1, 2017.

HB 1279 2017

PUERTO RICO

This law was written by Eyal Rosenstock, an attorney practicing in Maryland, and has been passed in Puerto Rico. He says the following about his law, which is included below in a translated version:

"The Law as far as I can tell, is one of the most advanced parent alienation laws in the world, and it only scratches the surface of what needs to be changed. It is advanced in the sense that it states that the conduct that leads to the child's rupturing of their emotional attachment to one of their parents is child abuse. So it informs the judge that this is serious, this is child abuse, and can damage the child permanently. Next it expressly provides a measure that allows for a psychological evaluation. (There is still a gap in parent alienation legislation: the child abuse laws need to be updated to include a clinically-informed definition of child abuse). Continuing on, the law includes several provisions for removal of custody if parent alienation is diagnosed.

This is a child protection law by nature, and provides custody if parent alienation is diagnosed as a form of protection for the abused child. So it provides real avenues of protection for a child, while also informing a judge, and the legal community, that this conduct is serious, whose conduct is so serious it can rise to the level of custody removal. So it almost serves as a protective order measure. (That is also a gap in the parent alienation law—it needs to be included in domestic violence protective order law—because parent alienation is ultimately a form of domestic violence, a brutal one. It leaves no obvious, visible imprints. However, if the brain were to be examined, strong imprints of trauma could be visible to the trained eye.)

Also, the law has an interesting provision in that if a parent is found to have been responsible for the psychological damage, that parent is responsible for the costs of therapy for the child.

(There is still a gap in parent alienation legislation: the child abuse law).

Next, it expressly provides a measure that allows for a psychological evaluation. In this respect, this can be huge for a case with parent alienation in that it has the potential to remove the case from the adversarial environment of a court litigation, into the therapeutic environment of a clinical evaluation.

Further legislation needs to include a release valve for courtroom litigants to go into parent alienation-informed clinical treatment and if a party does not follow treatment, the court can intervene.

LAW

To amend Articles 7 and 9 of Law 223-2011, known as the "Law Protecting the Rights of Minors in the Custody Award Process", in order to contemplate parental alienation in the custody determination; and for other related purposes.

STATEMENT OF MOTIVES

The family is the main protagonist in the upbringing and development of our minors. The family experience modulates and guides children through childhood and towards maturity, it is in the family where we can find explanations for the behavior and conduct of our minors. An adequate emotional and affective bond between parents and children translates into healthy family development for both. Unfortunately during the last decades we have seen changes in the family structure, this due to the increase in divorces or separations.

After a divorce or separation, as the case may be, and once custody of the sons and / or daughters has been established, the State guarantees the right of both minors and parents to relate and maintain the appropriate family tie. In this way, a regime of visits to the non-custodial parent is established; They have important psychological functions for the development of childhood, in addition to safeguarding the emotional bond between the child and her parents.

However, and even when the State guarantees the aforementioned right, there are occasions when one of the parties obstructs the filial relations of their sons and daughters with the other parent; in certain cases transforming the conscience of their children, through the use of different strategies, in order to prevent, obstruct or destroy their links with the other parent.

This behavior, known as parental alienation, originates mainly in the context of disputes over the custody and care of children. The effects of parental alienation on minors and the alienated parent are considered a variant of emotional and psychological abuse, being one of the most subtle forms of child maltreatment, which in turn can produce permanent psychological damage in the bond with the parent (a) alienated; as well as in the integral development of the minors involved.

Although there is no pattern applicable to all cases, important factors have been identified that alert to its presence. That is why the judicial determination must not be sustained in legal statements without the presence of specialists in human behavior. In most jurisdictions it is seen as a problem to be addressed through civil and non-criminal channels. The criminal process can place you in the uncomfortable situation of testifying to penalize one of your parents. Apart from this, the complexity of the alienating behavior presents a challenge for criminal legislation. We understand that custody determination and its subsequent evaluation in family court must be the most appropriate mechanism to address these situations and provide remedies that tend to advance the emotional health of the minor and strengthen family relationships as much as possible.

It is the public policy of the Government of Puerto Rico to ensure the best interest, protection, and comprehensive well-being of children and adolescents, and in the duty to ensure that well-being, reasonable opportunities and efforts must be provided to preserve family and community ties when it does not harm them. For this reason, this Legislative Assembly considers it necessary to update the definitions of this statute in order to continue effectively guaranteeing the well-being and protection of children on our island.

DECIDE BY THE LEGISLATIVE ASSEMBLY OF PUERTO RICO:

Section 1.- A new subsection (13) is added, and the current subsection (13) is renumbered as subsection (14), in Article 7 of Law 223-2011, to read as follows:

"Article 7.-Criteria to be considered in the custody award

When considering a custody application in which controversies arise between the parents regarding it, the court will refer the case, to the Social Unit of Family Relations, or to the licensed professional that it deems necessary, such as psychologists, psychiatrists, counselors or social workers, who will conduct an evaluation and report with recommendations to the court. Both the social worker or the licensed professional indicated above, when making their assessment, and the court, when issuing its determination, will take into account the following criteria:

(one) ...

(13) It will analyze the presence of parental alienation, or any other reasons that could cause the minor's resistance to relate to her parents. Parental alienation refers to the obstruction by one of the parents of the filial relationships of their sons or daughters, minors, with the other parent, through the use of different strategies, with the purpose of transforming or indoctrinating the conscience of their sons or daughters, in order to denigrate, prevent, obstruct or destroy their ties with the other parent and the minor presents thoughts or feelings of rejection to the other parent; demonstrates negative attitudes towards this or if, in effect, the affective bond between the minor and the other parent has been affected. All actions arising from this subsection must occur repetitively so that they constitute a pattern and not based on isolated events.

Parental alienation may be evidenced, without being understood as a limitation, in the following ways:

(i) Refuse to pass phone calls or attempt to direct the content of such calls to children.

(ii) Organize activities with the children during the period that the other parent should normally exercise their right to visit or find ways to hinder the reunion between them.

(iii) Intercept letters, messages or packages sent to the children.

(iv) Devaluate and insult the other parent in front of the children.

(v) Refusing to inform the other parent, on purpose, of the activities in which the children are involved, such as school, family, social or other functions.

(vi) Talk rudely about the new spouse of the other parent.

(vii) Prevent the other parent from exercising their visitation rights.

(viii) Make important, non-emergency decisions about children without consulting the other parent.

(ix) Change (or try to change) their surnames or first names.

(x) Prevent the other parent from accessing the children's school and medical records.

(xi) Go on vacation without the children and leave them with another person, even if the other parent is available and voluntary to take care of them.

(xii) Discredit the clothes or gifts that the other parent has bought them, and prohibit them from wearing them.

(xiii) Threatening children with punishment if they dare to call, write or contact the other parent.

(14) Any other valid or pertinent criteria that can be considered to guarantee the best welfare of the minor. "

Section 2.- Article 9 of Law 223-2011 is amended to read as follows:

"Article 9.-When joint custody will not be considered as beneficial and favorable for the best interests of minors.

Joint custody will not be considered as beneficial and favorable to the best interests of minors in the following cases:

If, after granting joint custody, one of the parents, recklessly, arbitrarily and unfairly refuses to accept said decision, and performs acts to hinder the relationship of the other parent with the minors, the court may alter the decree and grant custody to the other parent. Faced with the proposal of acts constituting parental alienation, the court may order an evaluation to the Social Unit of Family Relations or to the licensed professional that it deems necessary, such as psychologists, psychiatrists, counselors or social workers, who will prepare reports and present their findings and recommendations to the court. The court may, if deemed necessary, evaluate the parties or any other evidence it deems pertinent.

When evidence has been found that one of the parents has committed parental alienation, by the party that has custody of the minors, the court will evaluate the removal from custody or other precautionary measures at the discretion of the judge. If the parental alienation is committed by a relative, stepmother, stepfather or partner of the parent, the court will take measures to protect minors.

When you are a parent who engages in the conduct of parental alienation, the court will evaluate ordering psychological therapy as a protective measure prior to the decision of removal from custody. In case of ordering psychological therapies, the court will evaluate the progress of this to make new recommendations, if necessary and merit.

Any parent who causes emotional or psychological harm to minors by the behavior of parental alienation, will be ordered to pay for psychological therapies that entail the repair of such harm in minors.

The court will have the discretion to take the measures and issue the orders it deems pertinent at any stage of the process. "

Section 3.-This Law shall take effect immediately after its approval.

Appendix B

Further Reading

―――――――――――――――――――

$\mathcal{H}$ere, instead of the usual list of references, you'll find a collection of all the known books on parental alienation. There are two lists, which have been compiled by William Bernet, M.D. of the Parent Alienation Study Group, as a useful resource to help you further extend your understanding of PA. The first list includes book written by health and legal professionals, while the second list contains insightful books written by parents who have experienced PA.

SEVENTY-FIVE IMPORTANT BOOKS AND BOOK CHAPTERS REGARDING PARENTAL ALIENATION BY MENTAL HEALTH AND LEGAL PROFESSIONALS

William Bernet, M.D. — July 2020

This annotated bibliography regarding parental alienation includes books from fourteen countries—Argentina, Australia, Brazil, Canada, France, Germany, Italy, Mexico, Portugal, Spain, Sweden, Turkey, the United Kingdom, and the U.S.—which indicates the international scope of this serious form of child maltreatment. Most of these books were published within the last ten years. Most of the authors listed here are members of the Parental Alienation Study Group.

Jose Manuel Aguilar (2013). *SAP. Síndrome de Alienación Parental.* The author (from Spain) describes the process of one parent's manipulation of a child to reject the other parent without justification. This was the first book to explain this phenomenon, parental alienation, in Spanish.

Jane Appell (2006). *Divorce Doesn't Have to Be That Way: A Handbook for the Helping Professional.* This is a comprehensive guide to divorce counseling. Written specifically for helping professionals, the emphasis is on a family-centered, non-adversarial approach. One chapter is titled "Parental Alienation."

Niles-Göran Areskoug (2013). *Parental Alienation: A Swedish Perspective.* The author (from Sweden) described

214

a multigenerational case of parental alienation and how government authorities responded to it.

Amy J. L. Baker (2007). *Adult Children of Parental Alienation Syndrome: Breaking the Ties That Bind*. Baker was one of the first psychologists to conduct systematic research regarding parental alienation syndrome and parental alienation. In this research project, Baker collected the life stories of adults who had previously experienced parental alienation syndrome as children.

Amy J. L. Baker, Paul R. Fine, and Alianna LaCheen-Baker (2020). *Restoring Family Connections: Helping Targeted Parents and Adult Alienated Children Work through Conflict, Improve Communication, and Enhance Relationships*. Broken relationships between adult children and their parents are a widespread phenomenon. This book is a guide for therapists who aim to help their clients deal with those situations, especially when the cause was parental alienation.

Amy J. L. Baker and S. Richard Sauber (Eds.) (2013). *Working with Alienated Children and Families: A Clinical Guidebook*. Baker, Sauber, and their colleagues explained various interventions for families that experience parental alienation.

Amy J. L. Baker and Mel Schneiderman (2015). *Bonded to the Abuser: How Victims Make Sense of Childhood Abuse*. The authors explain how most abused children strive to maintain a "traumatic bond" with their abusive parent. In contrast, alienated children—who were never abused by their alienated parent—strongly reject those parents.

Siegfried Bäuerle and Helgard Moll-Strobel (Eds.) (2001). *Eltern sägen ihr Kind entzwei. Tren-nungserfahrungen und Entfremdung von einem Elternteil (Parents Saw Their Child in Two. Separation Experiences and Alienation from a Parent).* The editors (from Germany) invited several chapter authors to discuss psychological, social, and legal aspects of parental alienation.

William Bernet (Ed.) (2010). *Parental Alienation, DSM-5, and ICD-11.* In this book, Bernet and his colleagues methodically laid out the arguments that parental alienation should be recognized as a serious mental condition experienced by thousands of children and adolescents.

Wilfrid von Boch-Galhau (2013). *Parental Alienation and Parental Alienation Syndrome/Disorder: A Serious Form of Psychological Child Abuse.* The author (from Germany) relates the letters, case histories, and interviews of victims of parental alienation, which describe their life experiences and problems that persisted into adulthood.

Wilfrid von Boch-Galhau, Ursula Kodjoe, Walter Andritzky, and Peter Koeppel (Eds.) (2003). *Das Parental Alienation Syndrome (PAS).* The editors (from Germany) organized and published the proceedings of an important conference regarding parental alienation syndrome that took place at Frankfurt (Main), Germany, in 2002.

José Ignacio Bolaños Cartujo (2008). *Hijos alineados y padres alienados: mediación familiar en rupturas conflictivas (Aligned Children and Alienated Parents: Family Mediation in Conflicted*

Divorces). The author (from Spain) applies mediation in cases of conflicted separation and divorce, describing through theoretical concepts and numerous examples a model, a method, and techniques that facilitate intervention with these families. There is special attention to families whose members may be involved in a contentious judicial procedure.

José Maria Bouza (2015). *Obstrucción del vínculo de los nietos con sus abuelos* (*Obstruction of the Bond of Grandchildren with Their Grandparents*). The author (from Argentina) explains common questions and doubts regarding these relationships. The book discusses relevant modifications in the law in Argentina. It provides a typical schedule for visitation with grandparents.

Barry Bricklin (1995). *The Custody Evaluation Handbook: Research-Based Solutions and Applications*. The book explains psychological tests—such as the Bricklin Perceptual Scales and the Perception-of-Relationships Test—which may be helpful in identifying parental alienation in the context of a child custody evaluation.

Roland Broca and Olga Odinetz (Eds.) (2016). *Séparations Conflictuelles et Aliénation Parentale: Enfants en Danger* (*Conflicted Separations and Parental Alienation: Children at Risk*). The editors (from France) present a collection of authors who addressed clinical and legal aspects of parental alienation, as well as interventions. The book includes extensive literature reviews and case histories.

Janelle Burrill (2001). *Parental Alienation Syndrome in Court Referred Custody Cases*. This was an early quantitative research study regarding parental alienation. It found that the more negative behaviors a child exhibits toward an alienated parent, the more severe were the alienating parent's symptoms and behaviors.

Michael R. Bütz (2020). *Parental Alienation and Factitious Disorder by Proxy beyond DSM-5: Interrelated Multidimensional Diagnoses*. The author provides a new diagnostic framework for conditions such as factitious disorder by proxy and parental alienation.

Giovanni Battista Camerini, Marco Pingitore, John Lopez (2016). *Alienazione Parentale: Innovazioni Cliniche e Giuridiche (Parental Alienation: Clinical and Legal Innovations)*. The authors (from Italy) highlight the contributions of various writers allowing for scientific and methodological comparison, even with different points of view. They explain psychosocial solutions to be taken to counter parental alienation.

Adele Cavedon and Tiziana Magro (2010). *Dalla Separazione All'Alienazione Parentale: Come Giungere a Una Valutazione Peritale (From Separation to Parental Alienation: How to Reach an Expert Assessment)*. The authors (from Italy) explain how to identify or diagnose parental alienation with detailed case examples.

Craig Childress (2015). *An Attachment-Based Model of Parental Alienation: Foundations*. The author used established constructs and principles of psychology to describe the mental and interpersonal processes that constitute parental alienation.

Stanley S. Clawar and Brynne V. Rivlin (1991, 2013). *Children Held Hostage: Identifying Brainwashed Children, Presenting a Case, and Crafting Solutions.* In this research, which was commissioned by the Family Law Section of the American Bar Association, Clawar and Rivlin summarized their observations on 1,000 children from divorced families.

Brian L. Cutler and Patricia A. Zapf (Eds.) (2015). *APA Handbook of Forensic Psychology.* This is an encyclopedic, two-volume work published by the American Psychological Association. Marc J. Ackerman and Jonathan W. Gould contributed the chapter "Child Custody and Access," which has a section on "Child Alienation."

Douglas Darnall (2010). *Beyond Divorce Casualties: Reunifying the Alienated Family.* This book explains reunification therapy in detail, including: how to prepare for reunification; how to work with attorneys, mediators, and parenting coordinators; and even how to say "goodbye" if reunification is not possible.

J. Louise Despert (1953). *Children of Divorce.* Despert, a child psychiatrist, described the phenomenon of parental alienation more than 30 years before Richard Gardner introduced the term "parental alienation syndrome."

Robert A. Evans and J. Michael Bone (2011). *The Essentials of Parental Alienation Syndrome (PAS): It's Real, It's Here, and It Hurts.* The authors explain the manifestations of parental alienation and how to distinguish mild, moderate, and severe levels of this condition. They address controversies regarding parental alienation in an even-handed manner.

Leslie Drozd, Michael Saini, and Nancy Olesen (2012, 2016). *Parenting Plan Evaluations: Applied Research for the Family Court.* In this book, Michael Saini, Janet R. Johnston, Barbara Jo Fidler, and Nicholas Bala contributed the chapter "Empirical Studies of Alienation," which summarized and reviewed 58 published papers and doctoral dissertations regarding parental alienation.

Elizabeth M. Ellis (2000). *Divorce Wars: Interventions with Families in Conflict.* When parents divorce, children are the biggest losers. This book gives both mental health and legal professionals the information they need to help families navigate this grave ordeal and improve the outcome for hurting children. The author addresses the identification of parental alienation.

Sandra Inês Feitor et al. (2014). *Olhar analítico e subjective sobre as carências da intervenção e valências existentes no Sistema Português no âmbito da Alienação Parental* (*Analytical and Subjective Look at the Shortcomings of Intervention and Existing Valences in the Portuguese System in the Scope Of Alienation*). The authors (from Portugal and Brazil) address legal aspects, clinical features, and interventions for parental alienation in their respective countries.

Francisco José Fernández Cabanillas (2017). *Manual del Síndrome de Alienación Parental: claves para comprender el maltrato psicológico infantil en casos de divorcio: la situación en España* (*Manual of the Parental Alienation Syndrome: Keys to Understand Psychological Child Abuse in Divorce Cases: The Situation in Spain*). The author (from Spain) explores the hypothesis that children can be manipulated by one of their parents to hate and reject the other parent. This text is intended for magistrates, lawyers, doctors, psychologists, and educators who daily find themselves with these situations.

Barbara Jo Fidler, Nicholas Bala, Rachel Birnbaum, and Katherine Kavassalis (2008). *Challenging Issues in Child Custody Disputes: A Guide for Legal and Mental Health Professionals.* The authors (from Canada) discuss many clinical and legal aspects of disputes regarding parenting time for children of divorce. The book features a chapter "Understanding Child Alienation and Its Impact on Families."

Barbara Jo Fidler, Nicholas Bala, and Michael A. Saini (2012). *Children Who Resist Postseparation Parental Contact: A Differential Approach for Legal and Mental Health Professionals.* The authors (from Canada) provide an empirically based review of parental alienation, which integrates the best research evidence with clinical insight from interviews with leading scholars and practitioners.

Richard A. Gardner (1992). *The Parental Alienation Syndrome: A Guide for Mental Health and Legal Professionals.* In this seminal work, Gardner described in a comprehensive manner parental alienation syndrome, the mental condition that he had previously conceptualized and named in 1985.

Richard A. Gardner (2001). *Therapeutic Interventions for Children with Parental Alienation Syndrome.* The purpose of the book was to provide therapists with techniques to reintegrate alienated children with their rejected parents. It is only by deprogramming and other therapeutic interventions that there is any hope for the child's rapprochement with the alienated parent.

Richard A. Gardner, S. Richard Sauber, and Demosthenes Lorandos (Eds.) (2006). *The International Handbook of Parental Alienation Syndrome: Conceptual, Clinical and Legal Considerations*. At the time of its publication, this was the most wide-ranging book available regarding parental alienation syndrome. It included 34 chapters written by 31 authors from eight countries.

Carla B. Garrity and Mitchell A. Baris (1994). *Caught in the Middle: Protecting the Children of High-Conflict Divorce*. The authors emphasize that early intervention is important in cases of parental alienation. They explain how parenting coordination and other interventions may be very helpful.

Christine Giancarlo (2018). *Parentectomy: A Narrative Ethnography Of 30 Cases of Parental Alienation And What To Do About It*. The author says children come first and need both parents. Based on a peer-reviewed research study, this book relates, in their own voices, the stories of thirty loving, capable, and dependable parents who were removed from their children's lives.

Linda J. Gottleib (2012). *The Parental Alienation Syndrome: A Family Therapy and Collaborative Systems Approach to Amelioration*. Gottleib explains how techniques from structural family therapy can be used to heal the relationship between the child and the alienated parent. The book includes case vignettes and many quotations from alienated children, favored parents, and rejected parents.

Lyn R. Greenberg, Barbara J. Fidler, and Michael A. Saini (Eds.) (2019). *Evidence-Informed Interventions for Court-Involved Families: Promoting Health Coping and Development.* The authors (from Canada) explain a variety of interventions that can be used with families that manifest resist/refuse dynamics.

Guglielmo Gullotta, Adele Cavedon, and Moira Liberatore (2008). *La sindrome da alienazione parentale. Lavaggio del cervello e programmazione dei figli in danno dell'altro genitore* (*Parental Alienation Syndrome. Brainwashing and Programming Children to Harm the Other Parent*). The authors (from Italy) provide a systematic description of parental alienation and its manifestations, with a discussion of the differential diagnosis and related topics such as false memories and factitious disorder by proxy.

Linda Gunsberg and Paul Hymowitz (Eds.) (2005). *A Handbook of Divorce and Custody: Forensic, Developmental, and Clinical Perspectives.* The editors collected chapters from many authors regarding clinical and legal aspects of divorce and child custody. Moisy Shopper contributed the chapter on parental alienation.

Janet Haines, Mandy Matthewson, and Marcus Turnbull (2020). *Understanding and Managing Parental Alienation: A Guide to Assessment and Intervention.* The authors (from Australia) delivered a comprehensive look at how parental alienation begins, develops, and resists attempts at intervention.

Jennifer Jill Harman and Zeynep Biringen (2016). *Parents Acting Badly: How Institutions and Societies Promote the Alienation of Children from Their Loving Families.* The authors addressed how parenting stereotypes, gender inequality, and social institutions (such as family courts) sanction and even promote the problem of parental alienation.

Lena Hellblom Sjögren (1997). *Hemligheter och minnen: Att utreda tillförlitlighet I sex ualbrottmå* (*Secrets and Memories: Investigating Reliability In Sexual Offenses*). The author (from Sweden) explained how psychologists can investigate allegations of child sexual abuse. In two of the case examples, the analysis involved parental alienation. Those comments were the first explanations of parental alienation published in Swedish.

Lena Hellblom Sjögren (2013). *Barnets rätt till familjeliv: 25 svenska fallstudier av föräldraalienation* (*The Child's Right to Family Life: 25 Swedish Case Studies of Parental Alienation*). The author (from Sweden) explained that in some cases the alienating parent enjoyed support from social authorities and from the legal system. Parental alienation violates the child's legal right to family life. Twenty-five Swedish cases of severe parental alienation were presented.

Marie-France Hirigoyen (2012). *Abus de Faiblesse et Autres Manipulations* (*Abuse of Weakness and Other Manipulations*). The author (from France) explains how manipulation is the abuse of influence over another person, the targeting and exploiting of another's emotional and mental weaknesses. One of the manipulation vignettes in the book pertains to parental alienation.

Daniel J. Hynan (2014). *Child Custody Evaluation: New Theoretical Applications and Research.* The author, who has conducted many child custody evaluations, described his methodology in detail. The book includes a chapter on "Parental Alienation and Gatekeeping."

Janet R. Johnston and Vivienne Roseby (1997). *In the Name of the Child: A Developmental Approach to Understanding and Helping Children of Conflicted and Violent Divorce.* The authors explain parental alignments and alienation among children of high-conflict divorce, and how children of different developmental periods may be affected.

Ashish Joshi (2020). *Parental Alienation: A Handbook for Family Law Practitioners.* This book helps family law attorneys and court-appointed professionals understand the phenomenon of parental alienation. It provides tips on effectively litigating parental alienation and related issues.

Abigail M. Judge and Robin M. Deutsch (Eds.) (2017). *Overcoming Parent–Child Problems: Family-Based Interventions for Resistance, Rejection, and Alienation.* The chapter authors addressed conceptual, clinical, and empirical views of parental alienation. They explain a particular intervention called Overcoming Barriers.

Florence W. Kaslow (2013). *Divorced Fathers and Their Families: Legal, Economic, and Emotional Dilemmas*. Kaslow—an important leader of the American Psychological Association—related the stories of divorced fathers who were forced out of the lives of their children. They addressed both common and unusual problems that fathers face, including parental alienation.

Joan Kloth-Zanard (2009). *Where Did I Go Wrong? How Did I Miss the Signs? – Dealing with Hostile Parenting and Parental Alienation*. This book, which was written without technical jargon, is intended for parents and also for mental health and legal professionals who deal with high-conflict relationships. The author included many clinical vignettes from her work with alienated families.

Edward Kruk (2013). *The Equal Parent Presumption: Social Justice in the Legal Determination of Parenting After Divorce*. The author (from Canada) emphasizes that it is vitally important for children to maintain meaningful relationships with both parents after divorce. This book presents an evidence-based framework of equal parental responsibility as the most effective means of shielding children from ongoing parental conflict and family violence.

Jay L. Lebow (2018). *Treating the Difficult Divorce: A Practical Guide for Psychotherapists*. The author describes strategies for therapists on how to calm individuals, couples, and families in acute distress, and help ease the transition to a new family structure. Chapters offer adaptations for different types of divorce, including high-conflict cases involving parental alienation.

Ken Lewis (2009). *Child Custody Evaluations by Social Workers: Understanding the Five Stages of Custody*. The profession of social work has played a critical role in conceptualizing and implementing child custody evaluations. This work by a veteran social worker is intended for social work practitioners and legal professionals seeking guidance for best practices in conducting mental health evaluations that serve the goal of promoting the optimal development of children and families.

David L. Levy (1943). *Maternal Overprotection*. This book—based on research at the Institute for Child Guidance in New York City in the 1930s—includes the earliest description in the clinical literature of parental alienation phenomena.

Demosthenes Lorandos and William Bernet (Eds.) (2020). *Parental Alienation – Science and Law*. This book develops three themes: guidance for clinicians and forensic practitioners on how to identify and treat parental alienation; detailed analysis on how the concept of parental alienation fulfills Daubert and Frye criteria for testimony in court; and rebuttal of misinformation regarding parental alienation.

Demosthenes Lorandos, William Bernet, and S. Richard Sauber (Eds.) (2013). *Parental Alienation: The Handbook for Mental Health and Legal Professionals*. The editors developed the most comprehensive book published up to that time regarding parental alienation. It contains chapters on the phenomenology of parental alienation, the assessment of contact refusal, interventions for various levels of parental alienation, legal strategies, and international aspects of parental alienation.

L. F. Lowenstein (2007). *Parental Alienation: How to Understand and Address Parental Alienation Resulting from Acrimonious Divorce or Separation.* The author (from the United Kingdom) provides an overview of parental alienation and parental alienation syndrome. There are sections on the role of the judiciary and treatment methods for parental alienation syndrome.

Doménec Luengo and Arantxa Coca (2007). *Hijos manipulados tras la separación cómo detectar y tratar la Alienación Parental* (*Children Manipulated After Separation – How to Detect and Treat Parental Alienation*). The authors (from Spain) explain how parental alienation and familial conflict affect each family member—especially the children—over time. The book also explores the most common causes of alienation and healthy, effective ways for the alienated parent to recover their bond with their children.

Homer B. Martin and Christine B. L. Adams (2018). *Living on Automatic: How Emotional Conditioning Shapes Our Lives and Relationships.* The authors introduced the concept of emotional conditioning, including how it occurs and becomes entrenched in our minds. They used parental alienation as an example of a maladaptive outcome of emotional conditioning.

Alejandro Mendoza Amaro and Alejandro Heredia Ávila (Eds.) (2020). *Aliención e Interferencia Parental* (*Alienation and Parental Interference*). The editors (from Mexico) assembled chapter authors from several Latin American countries to create a comprehensive book regarding parental alienation. The text addresses human rights and legal rights, domestic violence, judicial approaches, manifestations of alienation, the forensic evaluation, transgenerational features, legislation, and other topics.

Monica K. Miller, Jared Chamberlain, and Twila Wingrove (Eds.) (2014). *Psychology, Law, and the Wellbeing of Children*. This book is part of the American Psychology-Law Society Series. R. Brian Howe and Katherine Covell contributed the chapter "Parental Alienation and the Best Interests of the Child."

Asunción Molina Bartumeus, Asunción Tejedor Huerta, et al. (2013). *Programa de intervención para victimas de interferencias parentals' (PIVIP)* (*Intervention Program for Victims of Parcentale Interference*). The authors (from Spain) described a program, the PIVIP, that aims to preserve children from conflict and parental alienation, offering them adaptive and protective strategies, while helping parents be aware of the harm they can cause to their children and offering them resources to improve their parental role.

Marco Pingitore (2019). *Nodi e snodi nell'alienazione parentale: Nuovi strumenti psicoforensi per la tutela dei diritti dei figli* (*Knots and Joints in Parental Alienation: New Psycho-forensic*

Tools for the Protection of Children's Rights). The author (from Italy) dealt with parental alienation through a new point of view: that of the child and how it perceives itself, the father, and mother. Two innovative themes are addressed: psychological support for parents rejected by their children and treatment programs for the recovery of the broken relationship between the child and the rejected parent.

Gérard Poussin and Elizabeth Martin-Lebrun (1997). *Les Enfants du Divorce: Psychologie de la Separation Parentale.* The authors (from France) explained the psychological consequences of parental separation on the child and how family mediation and individualized aid may attenuate those consequences. The book also included a comparison of the results of studies conducted over the last twelve years.

Ronald P. Rohner and Abdul Khaleque (Eds.) (2005). *Handbook for the Study of Parental Acceptance and Rejection.* This book explained a psychological test, the Parental Acceptance–Rejection Questionnaire, which has been 99% accurate in distinguishing severely alienated children from nonalienated children.

Mark D. Roseman (2018). *Preserving Family Ties: An Authoritative Guide to Understanding Divorce and Child Custody, for Parents and Family Professionals.* The author's goal was to give a clearer understanding of the complexity in child custody when parents separate. This book offers parents and professionals the context in which the new reality unfolds.

Lynn Steinberg, Ph.D. (2020). *You're Not Crazy, Overcoming Parent/Child Alienation.* Expert witness in PA, guides alienated parents through the process of saving their relationship with their children and the legal process all while educating any uninformed courts, family law lawyers, DCFS, and evaluators about the signs of PA and the devastating effects it has on the children.

Asunción Tejedor Huerta (2015). *El Síndrome De Alienación Parental: Una Forma De Maltrato.* The author (from Spain) exposed parental alienating behaviors as a form of child abuse with detrimental psychological consequences. She also suggested methods of intervention to prevent further psychological strain on the children.

Fuat Torun (2017). *Ebeveyne Yabancılaşma Sendromu (Parental Alienation Syndrome).* The author (from Turkey) addressed this book to divorce lawyers, family court judges, social workers, forensic experts, scholars, psychological counselors, guidance experts, and psychiatrists. The book explains how a child who is programmed may develop parental alienation.

Núria Vázquez Orellana, Asunción Tejedor Huerta, et al. (2018). *Manual de coordinación de parentalidad: Abordaje de las familias con hijos atrapados en rupturas conflictivas (Parenting Coordination Manual: Addressing Families with Children Caught in Conflictive Ruptures).* The authors (from Spain) explain how parenting coordination, a novel intervention in their country, may help parents who have been blinded by pain or anger become good mothers and fathers.

Judith S. Wallerstein and Sandra Blakeslee (1989). *Second Chances: Men, Women, and Children a Decade after Divorce.* The authors used the "Medea syndrome" to describe parents who want revenge on their former wives or husbands, and to accomplish it by destroying the relationship between the other parent and the child.

Richard A. Warshak (1999). *Parental Alienation Syndrome in Court.* This monograph, originally prepared as a chapter for a manual on expert witness testimony published by the State Bar of Texas, examines parental alienation syndrome from a social science and legal perspective. Though written for attorneys, expert witnesses will also find it valuable in preparing for testimony and anticipating cross-examination.

Karen Woodall and Nick Woodall (2017). *Understanding Parental Alienation: Learning to Cope, Helping to Heal.* The authors (from the United Kingdom) intend this book for both parents and practitioners. The book discusses the causes of parental alienation, the manifestations of this serious mental condition, and interventions that are likely to be helpful in the short term and the long term.

Nelson Zicavo Martinez (Ed.) (2016). *Parentalidad y divorcio: (des)encuentros en la Familia latinoamericana (Parenting and Divorce: (Dis)encounters in the Latin American Family).* A group of professionals (from Argentina and other Latin American countries) unravel the progress, conflicts, and limitations regarding parenting and divorce. The book addresses domestic violence and the mistreatment suffered by those children who often get caught up in conflicts of parents who aspire to win a battle.

BOOKS WRITTEN BY EXPERTS AND PARENTS WHO HAVE EXPERIENCED PA

Kimber Adams (2009). *The Parentectomy: A Memoir: A Perspective on Rising above Parental Alienation.* This is an enlightening and heartrending depiction of the tactics involved in perpetrating parental alienation and the resilient courage of a mother determined to minimize the damage. This novel explores the multidimensional consequences of parental alienation and bond abuse—from the children's rejection of their loved and full-time mother to her anguishing decision and the encouraging events that follow.

Katherine C. Andre and Amy J. L. Baker (2015). *Getting Through My Parents' Divorce.* This workbook guides children amid divorce and parental conflict on how to understand, identify, and deal with the various difficulties that arise when parent's divorce and argue with each other. Some scenarios and topics include what to do when one parent tries to turn the children against the other parent and how to deal with emotional hardships during a divorce.

Rene Ashton (2009). *How to Stop Hating Your Ex So You Can Co-Parent in Peace.* A single mom takes us on her journey as she moves through the hatred towards her ex to how she created a step-by-step process to co-parent in peace.

Amy J. L. Baker, J. Michael Bone, and Brian Ludmer (2014). *The High-Conflict Custody Battle: Protect Yourself and Your Kids from a Toxic Divorce, False Accusations, and Parental Alienation.* This is a practical guidebook for people who are engaged in a high-conflict custody battle. The book provides helpful tips parents can use to defend themselves against false accusations and gives a realistic portrayal of what to expect during a legal fight.

Amy J. L. Baker and Paul R. Fine (2014). *Co-parenting with a Toxic Ex: What to Do When Your Ex-Spouse Tries to Turn the Kids Against You.* When caught in a loyalty conflict, children of divorced parents may become confused, conflicted, angry, anxious, or depressed. This book offers a positive parenting approach to dealing with a hostile ex-spouse.

Amy J. L. Baker and Paul R. Fine (2014). *Surviving Parental Alienation: A Journey of Hope and Healing.* Many divorces are high-conflict, involving allegations of abuse and chronic disagreements regarding parenting schedules. Some children become aligned with one parent against the other. This book features true stories and information about parents who have reconnected with their lost and stolen children, and offers insight and understanding into what exactly parental alienation is and how to handle it.

Alec Baldwin and Mark Tabb (2008). *A Promise to Ourselves: A Journey through Fatherhood and Divorce.* After the author, a successful actor, and his wife divorced, the custody battle surrounding their daughter was the subject of media attention for years. Alex Baldwin became concerned about how noncustodial parents are often forced to abandon hopes of access to their children. One chapter of the book is "Parental Alienation."

Elissa P. Benedek and Samantha A. Huettner (2020). *Divorce and Co-parenting: A Support Guide for the Modern Family.* This book addresses the full range of problems that divorcing parents face. The author, a former president of the American Psychiatric Association, says, "The custodial parent has a legal—and we believe a moral—responsibility to see that the children spend time with their other parent." Parental alienation is discussed in two sections, "When Children Don't Want to Have Parenting Time" and "Dealing with Angry, Alienated Children."

William Bernet and Judge Don R. Ash (2007). *Children of Divorce: A Practical Guide for Parents, Therapists, Attorneys, and Judges.* The book blends the expertise of psychiatric and legal professionals, with the premise that children of divorce should have a good relationship with both parents. Parental alienation is addressed in the chapter, "Trying to Love Both Parents."

Jann Blackstone-Ford and Sharyl Jupe (2004). *Ex-Etiquette for Parents: Good Behavior after a Divorce or Separation.* The premise of the book is that when divorced parents make choices that are in the best interests of their children, they are likely to have a harmonious relationship with their former spouses. They point out that parental alienation syndrome and good ex-etiquette are at opposite ends of the spectrum in terms of parenting behaviors.

José Maria Bouza (2013). *Guía práctica de actuación ante el impedimento de contacto con los hijos (Practical Guide of Action Before the Impediment of Contact with Children).* The author (from Argentina) teaches divorced parents how to deal with the unknown world of legal issues. The book shows parents how to participate actively in the defense of their rights and those of their children.

Jenna Brooks (2015). *The Alienated Mother: Rebuilding Your Life after Your Children Have Rejected You.* This book is intended for women who are no longer in danger from an abusive relationship. It is designed to help those individuals find a way to live a meaningful life in spite of the pain of being alienated from their children.

JP Byrne and Brendan Byrne (2016). *Don't Hug Your Mother.* These two brothers (from Ireland) relate the difficulties they experienced when their parents separated. The book recounts episodes of their dark past in harrowing detail. It is a compelling, heart-breaking, and ultimately uplifting story of how two young boys grew up and learned to confront evil and follow their hearts.

Jean-Pierre Cambefort (2016). *Famille éclatée, enfants manipulés (Broken Family, Children Manipulated).* The author (a psychologist from France) relates a representative case of parental alienation. He identifies the warning signs of manipulation. The book helps the ostracized parent understand the situation, react to the child and his ex-partner, and preserve the bond with the child against everything, so that when he grows up he is free to love his two parents again.

Penny Cross (2000). *Lost Children: A Guide for Separating Parents.* The author (from the United Kingdom) addresses

various ways to help children deal with parental separation
and divorce. In particular she explains how to avoid parental
alienation, despite the fact that Family Courts in U.K. are
sometimes considered outmoded and in need of reform.

Douglas Darnall (1998). *Divorce Casualties: Protecting Your
Children from Parental Alienation.* This was an early book
that explained parental alienation to parents and also to
mental health and legal professionals.

Douglas Darnall (2008). *Divorce Casualties: Keeping Your
Children Close While You're Breaking Apart.* Some parents
consciously, blatantly, and even maliciously denigrate their
ex-spouse through negative comments and actions. The
result is a child full of hate, fear, and rejection toward an
unknowing and often undeserving parent. This book teaches
parents how to prevent or minimize the damaging effects
of alienating behaviors on their children.

Michelle Darné (2017). *Parent Deleted: A Mother's Fight
for Her Right to Parent.* The author found herself callously
erased from the lives of her children and also silenced
by the law. The book is a gripping tale of one non-
biological, lesbian mother's fight for her children. And it
is a courageous, disturbing, and necessary exposé of an
emergent social justice frontier: the rights of all children
to be with their parents.

Jill Egizii (2010). *The Look of Love.* After nearly twenty
years of marriage, Anna realizes she must get free from
her controlling spouse. In the process, she loses the only

thing that made escaping worthwhile, her children. Her once "normal" relationships with her son and daughter mysteriously sour. While facing the fight of her life, Anna realizes the true meaning of friendship and love.

Jill Egizii and Judge Michele Lowrance (2012). *Parental Alienation 911 Workbook.* This product is intended for anyone who wants to understand the facts about parental alienation. In particular, it is geared toward arming parents who wonder if they are experiencing alienation with all the information they need to make the best of a difficult, potentially inflammatory situation.

Jorge Luis Ferrari and Nelson Zicavo Martínez (2011). *Padres separados: Como criar juntos a sus hijos (Divorced Parents: How to Raise Their Children Together).* The authors (from Argentina) are concerned about the large number of sad children who are missing one of their parents; single parents coping alone with raising children; and parents deprived of their children. They offer both parents and professionals in the social and legal sciences the results of their studies, experiences, and research.

Kenneth Fox (2019). *At the Point of a Knife.* This is a real-life thriller about a doctor who invents an important laser technology and the legal conspiracy to steal his successful hi-tech start-up. By day, he has a successful career; by night, he lives with an increasingly mentally ill spouse. While all of this is ongoing, the family's two young children are being severely alienated against him by his wife.

Allan Freeman-Jones (2017). *Parental Alienation: A Loving Father's Lost Years.* In the space of four years Allan went from bachelor to alienated father. When it looked like Allan may have gained increased access to his son Timothy, Margaret played her trump card: the father was accused of sexually abusing his son. Investigations by the Department For Child Protection and the police concluded the allegations were unfounded. For the sake of his son's mental and emotional wellbeing, seeing it as his only realistic course of action, Allan exited his son's life.

Monica Giglio (2017). *Parental Alienation Survival Coach.* Parental alienation is a form of bullying, domestic violence, and psychological abuse. After devoting their lives to trying to prevent this tragedy, some parents who feel their lives have lost their meaning become withdrawn, passive, and suicidal. This book captures the feelings of shock, confusion, and helplessness that parents experience as they are pushed out of their children's lives, and their desperate struggle for education to understand what's happening.

Herman Gill (2015). *Mindful Child Custody: Thinking Outside the Child Custody Box.* This book provides a new compass for divorced parents navigating the murky waters of child custody litigation in the face of the increasing erosion of their constitutional rights. This is an account of what happens to alienated parents in their desperate attempts to save the developmental lives of their child and enforce their lawful parental rights.

Daniel Gottlieb (2012). *Listen to Me!!! Your Child and Your Divorce.* The author (a psychologist from Israel) has compiled expressions direct from the minds and hearts of children. All are direct quotes, completely real, taken from deep discussions in the psychologist's office. These verbatim testimonies make it easy for parents to better understand their children's emotional experiences throughout the process of divorce.

Jonathan Groner (1991). *Hilary's Trial: The Elizabeth Morgan Case: A Child's Ordeal in America's Legal System.* This book recounts a highly publicized custody case, which involved allegations of sexual abuse and, ultimately, abduction of the child from the U.S. to New Zealand. The author, a journalist and practicing lawyer indicts the legal system's bureaucracy and parents who promote personal interests at the expense of a child's.

Steven Hedlesky (2014). *Letters to Chloe: A Well Documented Case of Parental Alienation Syndrome.* The author is a physician, who lost his daughter's love when his ex-wife turned their child against him. He kept meticulous records during a three-year custody battle, so the book is a chronology of annotated excerpts from emails, court transcripts, discovery documents, and consult reports.

Gabriele ten Hövel (2003). *Liebe Mama, Böser Papa: Eltern-Kind-Entfremdung nach Trennung und Scheidung: Das PAS-Syndrom (Dear Mom, Bad Dad: Parent' Child Alienation after Separation and Divorce: The PAS Syndrome).* The author shows how, every year in Germany alone, around 20,000 children fall victim to the bitter struggles between the two parents. As a result of extreme influence, children often reject the "bad" parent and refuse to make contact. The aim of this startling book is to prevent parental alienation.

Cleland James (2016). *The Child Who Hates Her Father and the Mother Who Caused It.* This book relates the personal biography of a U.S. Marine, who has fought the system, and a mother, who has caused parental alienation syndrome against him, resulting in the adult child rejecting her father. False allegations were made, intending to drive a wedge between the author and his daughter.

Michael Jeffries and Joel Davies (2009). *A Family's Heartbreak: A Parent's Introduction to Parental Alienation.* This is the true story of one parent's struggle to maintain a normal, loving relationship with his young son. From the emotionally devastating actions of the child's other parent to a court system and mental health community ill-equipped to deal with this destructive family dynamic, this book is both an education in parental alienation and an eye-opening experience for parents who don't believe this could happen to them.

Richard Joseph (2014). *Abuse & Betrayal: The Cautionary True Story of Divorce, Mistakes, Lies and Legal Abuse.* The author relates a deeply personal account of his experiences with marriage, divorce, and the effects of his ex-wife's behavior. The book follows the couple from happy beginnings to their tumultuous divorce. Some passages describe his ex-wife's attempts at alienating him from his daughters. The book raises questions about the fairness of the divorce process in our country and speaks to the biases in the legal and judicial systems.

Joan Kloth-Zanard (2013). *Broken Family Bonds: Poems and Stories from Victims of Parental Alienation.* This book provides a collection of poems and stories written by real victims of parental alienation that show the psychological pain and damage caused by this pathological family dynamic.

Cara E. Koch (2020). *From Heartbreak to Healing: Resolving Parental Alienation.* When parental alienation occurs, the back-and-forth pattern of a child's wanting to be with the alienated parent and then bolting and avoiding contact is confusing, frustrating, and damaging for both parent and child. This book describes one parent's mercurial journey to stay connected against all odds.

Judge Michele Lowrance (2011). *The Good Karma Divorce: Avoid Litigation, Turn Negative Emotions into Positive Actions, and Get On with the Rest of Your Life.* This guidebook offers a concrete path to transforming painful experience into positive action. Judge Lowrance hopes that divorcing couples who apply the practices described in this book will avoid a divorce trial. Firmly entrenched in real-world applicability, the book is intended for people in any phase of a divorce, but also for psychologists, psychiatrists, attorneys, judges, and social workers.

A. Jayne Major (2002). *Creating a Successful Parenting Plan: A Step-By-Step Guide for the Care of Children of Divided Families.* This is a guide on how to successfully create a comprehensive parenting plan for parental custody in court. This book teaches parents everything they need to know about creating a solid case, including key legal terminology and specific, valid requests the court can act upon.

Rod McCall (2016). *For the Love of Eryk: Surviving Divorce, Parental Alienation and Life After.* The author shares his personal experience with parental alienation, which was so severe, it led to the death of his son Eryk. The boy was killed by the hands of his own mother when she lost her parental rights as the courts finally saw through her alienating behaviors. Through interviews of many parents as well as professionals in family law, the book is a powerful resource which can raise awareness, educate, and be a catalyst for change.

William McGee (2018). *Half the Child.* This book takes place over four consecutive summers in the lives of Michael and his son Ben. The novel chronicles the separation, divorce, custody battle, and abduction that threaten to tear apart father and son. With courts continually ruling against Ben's father, it remains uncertain if their bond will survive. Ultimately, they will write their own love story.

Catherine L. Meyer and Sally Quinn (1999). *They Are My Children, Too: A Mother's Struggle for Her Sons.* The author (from the United Kingdom) narrates a harrowing and heartbreaking true story of international child abduction by the wife of the former British ambassador to the United States. This book records the determination of one woman fighting for her children and of the inadequacy of current international laws against child abduction.

Gladys Monge (2013). *Madre sin Hijos, Hijos sin Madre (Mother without Children, Children without Mother).* The author (from Puerto Rico) says that the concept of parental alienation has often been misunderstood. It continues to be necessary to educate mental health professionals, legal practitioners, and the general public about parental alienation, which is a great hardship for many children, teenagers, and their parents.

Gladys Monge (2014). *Hijos Perdidos: Alienación Parental Es Abuso Infantil (Lost Children: Parental Alienation is Child Abuse).* The author (from Puerto Rico) explains how to understand and recognize parental alienation, a form of child abuse that is occurring worldwide. She reflects on her personal experience when she lost two sons through divorce and her struggle in the courts. Gladys Monge is a survivor of parental alienation.

F. Leonard Myers (2016). *Tears in the Rain.* Parental alienation is featured in the plot line of this novel. Ten years after her parents' bitter divorce, under the misguided direction of a vengeful, narcissistic father, Julia Webster terminated her relationship with her loving mother who had sacrificed so much to rescue her from an orphan's life in China. But Julia meets a psychologist determined to rescue her from a future caught in her father's abusive campaign.

J. K. Nation (2019). *Ex's & Oh's: Dealing with Parental Alienation and Healing through the Pain.* The author takes the reader through the journey of parental alienation, providing the tools needed to find joy, healing, and restoration in the darkest times. Parental alienation leads to depression, financial despair, and in some cases even suicide. The goal for *Ex's & Oh's* is to bring life, freedom, and restoration to individuals and families impacted by parental alienation.

Kathleen M. Reay (2011). *Toxic Divorce: A Workbook for Alienated Parents*. The author (from Canada) explains that high conflict between divorcing or divorced parents, including parental alienation phenomena, is a noteworthy risk factor for children and adolescents. This workbook is the first of its kind for alienated parents, providing the knowledge and understanding to personally deal with the ramifications of parental alienation.

P. A. Rent (2018). *How to Steal a Family*. The author (from the United Kingdom) explains that it is surprisingly easy to break a family if you are so minded, and stupendously hard to either stop it, get help if it happens to you, or fix it. Based on a true story, this book brings to life how easily is can happen and the damage that ripples out from those directly involved through families, friends, and generations.

Pamela Richardson and Jane Broweleit (2006). *A Kidnapped Mind: A Mother's Heartbreaking Story of Parental Alienation Syndrome*. The author (from Canada) related the true story of how her son Dash suffered from parental alienation at the hands of his father. Ms. Richardson spent years battling Dash's father, the legal system, their psychologist, the school system, and Dash himself to protect her son—first from his father, then from himself.

Pamela Roche and Maggie Allen (2014). *Broken Lives Broken Minds*. This book is about parental abduction and parental alienation. It exposes the flaws and loopholes in the Hague Convention and the dramatic rise in parental abduction in the last 10 years. It explains how parental alienation is poorly recognized in courts today, so injustices are endemic in the family law system, which involves judges, lawyers, psychologists, and court-appointed therapists.

Elisabeth Schmidt and Allard Mees (Eds.) (2006). *Vergiss, dass es Dein Vater ist! Ehemals entfremdete Kinder im Gespräch (Remember That It Is Your Father! Formerly Alienated Children in Conversation)*. The editors (from Germany) present the comments of four children, aged 15, 20, 28 and 34, talking about their parents' separation and the loss of their father. The conflict of separating parents and its effects on the inner and outer development of the affected children are shown from the perspective of these children. The editors confirm that children need both parents, regardless of whether they remain a couple or not.

Traci Slatton (2016.) *The Year of Loving.* This novel involves parental alienation in its story line. Sarah's world is crumbling. One daughter barely speaks to her and the other is off the rails. In the midst of her second divorce, two men come into her life: an older man who offers companionship and stability and an exciting younger man whose life is as chaotic as hers.

Vesta Spivakovsky (2018). *Громче, чем тишина (Louder Than Silence)*. This is the first book published in the Russian language regarding parental alienation. This book brings the problem of family kidnapping and parental alienation into the field of public discussion. The author has made her personal tragedy public in order to force the government to pay attention to the lack of legal mechanisms for resolving family conflicts.

Asunción Tejedor Huerta (2013). *Programa de Intervención para Victimas de Interferencias Parentales (Intervention Program for Victims of Parental Interference)*. The author (from Spain) provides material for children, victimized by parental alienation, and their parents in order to facilitate communication and expression between them and ultimately remedy the adverse consequences of parental alienation. The content includes methods to improve the parenting strategies in order to prevent further damage to the children.

Isabelle Vuistiner-Zuber (2019). *Protection de l'enfance: Lettre ouverte à tous ses acteurs (Child Protection: Open Letter to All Its Actors)*. The author (from France) advises divorced parents to: be attentive to one's own reactions following the break-up; give the children more attention; and know the structures and procedures that can provide support. This book emphasizes that it is necessary to obtain absolute respect for the right of children to be raised by both parents.

Judith S. Wallerstein and Sandra Blakeslee (2003). *What About the Kids? Raising Your Children Before, During, and After Divorce*. This comprehensive book for parents has a chapter, "Parent–Child Alignments." This chapter discusses parental alienation and various other reasons why a child might be reluctant to visit or have a relationship with a parent.

Richard A. Warshak (2001, 2010). *Divorce Poison: How to Protect Your Family from Badmouthing and Brainwashing*. The two editions of Warshak's book are the most widely read accounts of parental alienation in the world. The books have been published in the U.S., Croatia, Czechia, Finland, Japan, and Korea.

Richard A. Warshak and Mark Otis (2010). *Welcome Back Pluto: Understanding, Preventing, and Overcoming Parental Alienation.* This DVD shows children, teens, and parents how to get along better, gives practical tips about how to maintain positive feelings, and motivates children and parents to use these tips by demonstrating why it is so important for children and teens to love both their parents.

Monty Weinstein and Vickie Taylor (2018). *From the Mob to the Therapist's Chair.* The author grew up in a wealthy family that made its millions off the grid and most definitely illegally. In college, however, he became focused and devoted to strengthening the family unit. Ultimately, Dr. Monty became a marriage and family therapist, when he began to realize that some parents going through divorce were being severely alienated and children were being brainwashed and turned against the other parent.

Pamela Weintraub and Terry Hillman (2005). *The Complete Idiot's Guide to Surviving Divorce.* This is a comprehensive book that discusses legal issues, finances, child custody, parenting time schedules, and remarriage. The section pertaining to parental alienation is called "When a Parent is Maligned."

Karen Woodall and Nick Woodall (2014). *The Guide for Separated Parents: Putting Children First.* The authors (from the United Kingdom) explain that children living in separated family situations fare best when their relationship with each of their parents continues to be close. Using strategies such as parenting plans, scripted phone calls, and parenting meetings, this book enables parents to communicate effectively on the most important things in their children's lives.

Joep Zander (Ed.) (2009). *Verpasseerd ouderschap: Loyaliteitsmisbruik en Ouderverstotingssyndroom (Parenting Broken by PAS: Loyalty Abuse and Parental Alienation Syndrome)*. The editor and chapter authors (from the Netherlands) provide an overview of parental alienation. They address clinical and legal aspects of this condition, and also discuss major controversies.

About The Author

*T*rained in the Family Systems model, Dr. Steinberg is a mediator and expert witness who works with families, couples, groups, and individuals to achieve positive outcomes in court.

For more than forty years she has specialized in working with children and adults abused as children and regularly appears in courts as an expert on sexual abuse.

Her interest and background grew naturally to embrace the psychological abuse of parental alienation, which she has specialized in for the last ten years. She offers a four-day intensive family reunification program in Los Angeles for alienated parents and their alienated children. She is an expert witness in parental alienation in the Childrens' Court and Family Court, Civil and Administrative Court, and can also testify to the treatment of members of the alienated family and assist with preparation for court appearances.

Dr. Steinberg is passionate about raising awareness of parental alienation. She hopes that by doing so, this form of psychological abuse will become more widely understood, and the victims—both parents and children—will be better supported.

Acknowledgements

I am so thankful and appreciative of so many people, and do not mean to leave anyone out.

Thank you, firstly, to Ron Berglas, my dear friend and patient editor, who helped to make my book more complete and exciting.

My love and appreciation goes to the daughter of my heart, my niece Tara, who is always loving, wise, and encouraging. Thank you to all of the wonderful young women whose social worker I was—you have loved me, encouraged me, and applauded me throughout the devastation I have experienced over the last ten years.

I acknowledge all the alienated parents who have attended my support groups and consulted with me, inspiring me with their bravery and fortitude.

To my special friends, Everil Bell, Kathy Gronau, Nina DiGracia, Linda Gunsberg, amongst others who have been supportive and loving throughout the time I was writing this book, which was also the period during which my three brothers, Peter, Glen, and Willem passed away.

Thank you to all the experts in alienation who have been so caring and available to me, and who's support has been instrumental in assisting me to continually further my development and knowledge of PA. Thanks to my mother's PA group, Joan Kloth-Zanard, Xiaojie Zeng, Amanda Buxbaum, and Deborah Murdoch for their love and support.

My little dog, Bella, who stayed loyally and lovingly by my side through thick and thin for ten years deserves my eternal thanks, as does my therapist, Dr. Diane Fletcher, and my loving "helpers", Jonathon, Yesenia, and Amalia.

A special thanks to "Robin" who worked diligently to finish editing the book. She also added her personal knowledge about the court process. Despite constantly dealing with a parent who relentlessly attempts to alienate their child from her, take her to court, stalk, hack and harass her, she still made the time to get this information about parent alienation out to the public.

Finally, not least of all, I thank my assistants, who put up with my frustration and constant requests for technical help – Ramiro, Patrick, and Johnny.

And now . . . I am ready to write my next book. Throughout this process I realized I love to write and there is still so much more to say on the subject of parental alienation. So stay tuned!

Notes

CPSIA information can be obtained
at www.ICGtesting.com
Printed in the USA
BVHW031914210122
626808BV00005B/82